IT'S ALL THE SAME GAME

IT'S ALL THE SAME GAME

The Sports Fan's Guide to Success in the Stock Market

NEIL RINEHART

Miriam —
My best to one
of the best.
With gratitude,
Neil

VANTAGE PRESS
New York

Before making any investment desision, the advice of a qualified investment professional should be considered in order to determine the suitability of investment choices with regard for your personal goals and objectives.

Because of the risk inherent in any stock investment, there is no guarantee that the methods described herein will be profitable in specific applications. Thus, neither the author nor the publisher assumes liability for any losses that may be sustained by use of the methods described in this book, and any such liability is hereby expressly disclaimed.

The mention of any security herein is not intended to be an offer or solicitation for the purchase or sale of that security. In addition, the views expressed in this book are those of the author and do not represent the views of his employer, its officers, or its other employees.

FIRST EDITION

Published by Vantage Press, Inc.
516 West 34th Street, New York, New York 10001

Manufactured in the United States of America
ISBN: 0-533-14595-3

Library of Congress Catalog Card No.: 2003104795

0 9 8 7 6 5 4 3 2 1

Dedicated to all those we call

"coach."

Table of Contents

Acknowledgments ix

Introduction 1

Section I The Traits Of The Greats

Chapter 1: Discipline 5
Chapter 2: Confidence 17
Chapter 3: Focus 27
Chapter 4: Flexibility 37

Section II The Defense (A Meeting with the Defensive Coordinator)

Chapter 5: The Defensive Foundation 49
Chapter 6: Staying In The Game 61
Chapter 7: Fifty Was Once Ten 73
Chapter 8: The Nightmare Known As Negative Compounding 85

Section III The Offense (A Meeting with the Offensive Coordinator)

Chapter 9: The Offensive Foundation 95
Chapter 10: The Offensive Sweet Spot 111
Chapter 11: The Other Half Of Dual Analysis 119
Chapter 12: The "Elevator Offense" 135
Chapter 13: The Best Time To Invest 145
Chapter 14: The Second Time Around 157

Section IV The Special Teams (A Meeting with the Special Teams Coordinator)

Chapter 15: Special Teams and Special Approaches 169

Chapter 16: Your Portfolio Is Not One Big Emergency 179

Chapter 17: A Different Kind Of E.S.P. 189

Chapter 18: Was It Sports Or Sports Psychology? 205

Index 213

Afterword 217

Acknowledgments

Let me take this opportunity to acknowledge some very special people. First, to Mom and Dad, thank you for giving me your traditional values and a dose of classic midwestern good judgment.

Thank you to all the coaches and teachers who guided and encouraged me along the way, especially Larry Giles (high school baseball) and Merlin Wilkins (high school English).

I am grateful for all the truly professional business associates I have had the pleasure of working with, including Joe Sando, Miriam Kindred, and especially, Dan Wilhite.

A special debt of gratitude goes to Mary Webber. No one could ask for a better business partner, friend and advocate. Mary, you truly understand client service better than anyone I have ever known.

Allie, thanks for your constant faith in this project. Your confidence in me was unmatched, but never unappreciated. I know you will go far on life's journey,

Thank you, Matt. You are undoubtedly the number one sports fan in the family, and your straightforward critical reviews were invaluable. It is a pleasure watching your entrepreneurial spirit unfold.

Finally, thank you Sheila. You are my best friend, and will always be the love of my life. Your unfailing support for this project was a blessing, as you once again helped me realize my dreams. You are, and always will be, my best "fan."

They say that what really matters is not whether you won or lost, but how you played the game. I have always had a problem with that. Isn't the fact that you either won or lost one of the best ways to determine how you played the game?

Introduction:
The Pre-game Report

Other than my wife and children, the two passions in my life are sports and the stock market. Now a fifty-something, I decided that it was time to record my perspective regarding the rules of successful stock investing in a way that would connect with the true sports fan. By the way, my opinion is that sports fans are some of the most dedicated, passionate people in the world. I also believe that successful sports figures have an almost incomparable, off-the-charts way of dealing with the highs and lows along this journey we call life. With that in mind, this work is based on the premise that the inner "rules" and qualities of great sports figures can be invaluable to serious sports fans who would like to become more serious and successful as investors. By using sports analogies, sports talk, and historic capsules about great players and coaches, my goal is to help you identify with financial concepts from the fresh perspective of a sports fan. After all, I have been an investment professional, and a fan of the stock market, for over twenty-five years; but I have been a sports fan for over forty years.

It all started for me at age eight, when my father and grandfather took my brother and me on a day trip to see our first big league baseball game. The year was 1959, and the Yankees were in Kansas City to play the old Kansas City Athletics (believe it or not, Roger Maris was still a K.C. Athletic at that time). The historic drama of the 1961 home run race between Maris and Mantle was still to come. Anyway, on that sunny afternoon in 1959, I witnessed my first big league ballgame, and I was hooked. That day the women in the family went to see Elizabeth Taylor in some matinee movie. I don't even remember which team won the game that day, but I definitely know that the guys got the better end of the deal.

From that day on I was a sports fan. Fanatic—fan—call me what you will. You know what I mean because you are in the same camp. My hope is that you have some similar childhood memory that includes sunshine and summer days, or football and fall afternoons. Regardless, I hope it makes you smile when you think about it.

My other passion is investing in the stock market, and I have dedicated my professional career to that challenge for more than twenty-five years. In recent times the market has been a menacing yet magnetic topic. While some of the personal finance books available today are overly technical, and some are way too elementary, this one falls in the crease for the serious, yet hungry student of the markets. My sincere hope is that this playbook will become a valuable reference, like an assistant coach who is always on the sideline with you, over a long and profitable investment career.

SECTION ONE:
THE TRAITS OF THE GREATS

CHAPTER ONE:
DISCIPLINE

We make few rules. Those we make, we keep.

Vince Lombardi
Legendary NFL Coach

* * *

Nolan Ryan lost more games than 99% of the pitchers who ever pitched in the major leagues (292 losses). He also pitched seven no-hitters, struck out 5,714 batters, won 324 games, and was elected to the Hall of Fame in 1999.

Dan Marino threw 3,391 incomplete passes and 252 interceptions over a seventeen year career with the Miami Dolphins (both are league records). He also connected for over 61,000 passing yards and 420 touchdowns, more than any other quarterback in the history of the NFL.

John Wooden was involved with basketball as a player and coach for thirty-five years . . . thirty-five . . . before winning his first NCAA Championship. Then, in an unmatched streak of superiority, his UCLA team won the national title ten times in twelve years (1964-1975).

Reggie Jackson struck out 2,597 times in his big league career, more than any other player to ever play the game. He also hit 563 home runs, is ranked as the seventh best home run hitter of all time, and was elected to the Hall of Fame in 1992.

* * *

After personal setbacks like those experienced by these men, what are the special character traits that powered them on to greatness? What is it about the world's elite athletes and coaches? Just what is it that sets them apart from the rest of the pack?

A case can be made that the great ones in sports possess superior, all-pro levels of four character traits not generally found in common man, qualities we all know as:

1. discipline; 2. confidence;
3. focus; and 4. flexibility.

For the sports fan, the number four takes on a special significance; the foursome in golf, four quarters in football, four bases on a ball diamond, and four plays in a series of downs are just a few examples. Great players who wore #4 on their backs include Bobby Orr (Bruins), Duke Snider (Dodgers), Lou Gehrig (Yankees), and Bret Farve (Packers). As you focus on the number four, and four of the character traits that we all admire in great athletes, you can build on those traits to become a more successful stock market investor. We will explore some of the great minds in sports history, both players and coaches, and dig deeper into the discipline, confidence, focus, and flexibility that made them great. You will find comfort in the fact that this work is not presented in high-powered financial jargon, but rather from the perspective of the sports enthusiast. Whether you are a novice or an intermediate investor, this perspective and this playbook-like system can take you to a higher level of investment success.

* * *

One of the dominant traits that separates the successes from the failures in sports, in the stock market, and in life, is discipline. We know that discipline starts in that area above the neck and between the ears, with mental training that begins to mold our behavior before we ever realize it, but what is it that makes discipline so important in both the sports world and the investing world?

A great athlete like Kobe Bryant or Alex Rodriguez has a high level of natural skill at birth, but that talent can be wasted if the athlete doesn't have a high level of discipline to go along with his talent and his training. Most athletes with moderate talent can improve on their own for a while, but they eventually reach a level where they must have the help of others who have gone before them. Maybe that's why you picked up this book. You are at a point in your financial growth where you want some assistance from a financial coach to take you to the next level of understanding and discipline.

A successful teacher is surpassed by his students.

Anonymous

In the case of many exceptional athletes, (Tiger Woods, Cal Ripken, Peyton Manning), the great disciplinarian during the early years was the athletic father. With other great ones, there was usually a coach or teaching mentor that came along a little later in life that helped make the difference. This book will explore the simple truths found in the mental makeup of those athletes, both legendary and contemporary, that give us a model for our own real world success.

When you think of what makes your favorite sports star shine, you may first think of hand-eye coordination, or quick reflexes. While these are reasonable answers, many authorities would tell you that discipline is the single most important trait shared by truly great athletes of any era. We will go on to make the case that discipline is one of the most important traits shared by truly great investors, past and present.

* * *

He didn't even start playing the game in an organized way until he was thirteen years old. After all, there were plenty of other things to do in a small midwestern town in the sixties. But then it happened. He discovered basketball, and over time, he developed a love affair with the sport that would change his life. Over the next twenty-five years, he would go on to set college scoring records, play in a NCAA finals game, and help his team win three NBA Championships. In the 1980s, when the NBA was in need of heroes and role models, Larry Bird became a great ambassador for the sport of basketball. Even for those who were not Celtics fans, he was a special pleasure to watch every time he stepped on the court. Even today, if sports experts are asked to name true sports heroes who exemplified discipline and the will to prepare, Larry Bird's name is almost always on the list.

Larry Bird was not very fast and his ability to jump was not all that great. Nevertheless, he was blessed with a six foot, nine inch frame, and he had a mindset and a level of personal discipline that was off the charts. He improved on the things he could control, such as his understanding of basketball strategy, and his robotic shooting style. Was he a legend? Probably. Was he a disciplined professional? Absolutely.

With the proper training, the mind can become a calm, cool foundation for physical excellence. With the proper mental training, great athletes and coaches develop and nurture an unmatched level of trust in their own instincts. Regardless of the turmoil around them, they recognize that noise is noise, and they dial it down when they need to. Many million-dollar athletes use sandlot techniques to help ground them and put them in a disciplined frame of mind. If you don't believe that, think about the childlike ritual that an all-Star hitter like Nomar Garciaparra goes through as he steps up to the plate. All of those antics, many carried over from his early days in youth baseball, help him dial up a disciplined mindset that gives him the greatest chance of success at that moment. His preparation and discipline lead him to totally trust his hitting instincts, regardless of the heat of the situation. Whether we're looking at top of the first, with one out, in a spring training game; or bottom of the ninth, with a runner on second, in a pennant-race game, a similar level of mental discipline is evident.

The Year was . . .?

Celtics over Rockets for the NBA Championship
Home Depot goes public
MTV premieres
Microsoft is chosen to provide operating system for the IBM PC
Cal Ripken Jr. becomes a starter for the Baltimore Orioles
Oakland defeats Philadelphia in the Super Bowl
Dow Jones Industrial Average closes at 875

The year was . . . 1981.

When it comes to the great coaches, discipline often starts with rules bound in a three-ring binder that don't become meaningful until the players begin to believe in them. Vince Lombardi, in the eyes of many football historians, was one of the great disciplinarians of all time, and he certainly was one of the great professional football coaches of the twentieth century. His quote, "we make few rules, but those we make, we keep," was a perfect example of his no-nonsense approach.

Fundamentals, conditioning, and discipline were the hallmark of Vince Lombardi's style, and he maintained that approach to the game even though he did not become a successful NFL coach until he had made stops along the way at St. Celecia High (New Jersey), Fordham University, and West Point. Some of his players thought he treated them like animals, but all of his players respected him. Finally, after eighteen years of coaching at lower levels, his formula made the Green Bay Packers the team of the 1960's, and he became the winningest NFL head coach of all time (74% winning percentage). He knew that experience could only be deposited like cash, as it was earned, and players who did not buy into his philosophy of disciplined preparation and commitment usually didn't survive in the Lombardi system. It was as simple as that.

We are what we repeatedly do. Excellence, then, is not an act, but a habit.

Aristotle
Greek Philosopher

Excellence is not an act, but a habit. Somehow, I think that Lombardi and Aristotle would have enjoyed having dinner together. Later in his life, Coach Lombardi would acknowledge his devotion to discipline and commitment with the following quote, which he often used in speeches to the public:

The quality of any man's life has got to be a full measure of that man's personal commitment to excellence and to victory.

Vince Lombardi
Legendary NFL Coach

In the world of investing, discipline means having a defined plan that measures the potential risk and reward that may result from specific future events. It means having a methodology, much like a playbook, that includes a specific action to take based upon your view of a specific set of financial variables. This market playbook we will unlock is based on a predetermined set of rules, so that the methodology remains constant, regardless of the flow of events around you. It remains constant, no matter what your gut feeling is, and no matter what the guys on the cable news network are saying. The methodology, founded on a commitment to risk-management and defense, is all too often viewed as dull and boring by others around you who would rather think about the excitement of the "offense." Not so.

If you cheat on the practice field, you'll cheat in the game. And if you cheat in the game, you'll cheat the rest of your life.

Vince Lombardi

In analyzing the world of money and the markets, many investment professionals would say that the "defensive" coach has a greater chance of being successful over a long career than the "offensive" coach. Let's explore why. Any successful defensive coach has spent a tremendous amount of time developing an ability to react to constantly changing offensive sets and formations. Like an experienced fighter pilot, he has a plan for every contingency, so that he doesn't have to analyze and agonize over what to do in a real world situation when time is at a premium. That predefined playbook concept is one that will become increasingly meaningful to you as we continue this journey.

We will explore in depth one of the most fundamental rules in this playbook of investing, defined as "cut your losses." If an investor has the discipline to do this one simple thing consistently, then he can greatly increase his odds of being successful over time. Like avoiding turnovers in the world of football, it's almost as simple as "if I watch my backside, and take care of the downside, the upside will take care of itself." While this approach may not seem exciting enough for some, the great ones—great coaches, athletes, and investors—are disciplined enough to realize that we all make mistakes, in athletic games, in money games, and in life. What then, really separates the winners from the losers? When you break it down, it oftens seems that while we all make mistakes, winners make small mistakes, while losers make huge ones. This may not sound like much of a difference, but trust me, the difference is significant. Small miscues are okay, as long as you don't let small mistakes compund into large losses.

* * *

It was not "prime time." In fact, the small college he attended in Mississippi was Division 1-AA, with a total enrollment of less than three thousand students. He was 6′ 2″ with a lot of raw talent, which was enough to make him an early NFL draft pick in 1985. He had the hands of a wide receiver, but there was still no guarantee that he would become a career player, let alone a legend. When given the opportunity to improve toward excellence, his work ethic and discipline helped take him over the top. He practiced stair drills and pass-routes like a maniac, and he studied films of other wide receivers for hours on end. The result is that Jerry Rice, Mississippi Valley State graduate, became the all-time NFL career leader in touchdowns, receptions, and pass-reception yardage. In 1995, he had the honor of being named to the seventy-fifth anniversary All-NFL Team, and he is, arguably, the greatest wide receiver of all time. Rice had talent coming out of college, but what only became apparent later on was his special level of intense discipline. There is already a place waiting for him in Canton, Ohio.

In football, the strategy some coaches now use of pre-scripting the first few series of plays before the game begins is an example of how sports discipline often includes a perspective that is bigger than any one play or any one player. We will explore defined, pre-scripted ways to buy into an initial stock position that are not dependent on emotion or minute-by-minute analysis. If your goal is to invest a specific percentage of your portfolio in a specific stock, you will learn an "elevator system" of scaling into a stock that is based upon a fixed formula. This method will give you confidence and control, no matter how murky and mixed the market seems to be. An overview of this formula-driven approach is as follows:

If stock in company QQQ meets your draft (buy) criteria, buy X % (1/3 of your total desired position.)

If it goes down Y % from buy point, sell to limit your loss.

On the other hand, if it goes up Z % from you first buy point, buy another X %.

If it goes down Y % from second buy point, sell to limit your loss.

If it goes up another Z % from your second buy point, buy another X % to round out your position.

This unemotional, "elevator system" of buying stocks will become more meaningful and comfortable to you as we review it in detail in later sections of this book. As a key component of your investment playbook, it will give you confidence in your ability to react, no matter how the first few plays of the investing game unfold.

In the stock market, discipline means monitoring action that might attack your portfolio from different angles and different perspectives. For the successful investor, discipline often evolves into a predetermined blend of economics, psychology and statistics that takes form in his investing "playbook." Any successful head coach has developed a playbook based upon experience, probabilities, and real-game success ratios. The book includes well thought out plays and formations for specific situations, but it never includes a section called "second-guessing." Sure, there will always be Monday-morning quarterbacks who question a specific play in a specific situation, but they are of little concern to the disciplined, confident coach.

* * *

The wonderful thing about baseball is that you can enjoy it as a casual observer, and you can also enjoy it as a baseball graduate student who gets into the detailed chess-like reasoning behind each strategic move. Even though you won't see it in print, the infamous "book" on the unwritten rules of baseball includes specific strategies in specific situations that, over thousands of games played, have become precedent in determining how baseball experts measure success and failure.

In baseball, one of the rules in the book is "never make the first out of an inning at third base." Another example is "use a right-handed hitter over a left-handed hitter in a late game situation against a left-handed pitcher." This rule exists because of the time-tested, statistical fact that against left-handed pitchers, right-handed hitters have a higher probability of getting a base hit. This advantage, based upon the physics of a body in motion, is recognized as a simple fact of the game, but it is based upon thousands upon thousands of specific trials. That's how it got into the book in the first place. Simple strategies taken right out of the book seem so elementary to the baseball purist, but when chained together they can make the difference between winning and losing. Managerial discipline can give any team a higher probability of success, not only in one close game, but also over the course of a long season or a longer career. Like the book on baseball that is used by managers every day, my hope is that this book will help you dig deeper into the ways of the disciplined investor and increase your probability of long-term investment success.

What defines a successful general, or a successful military leader? Isn't he a coach who has developed discipline and commitment through dedication, training, and experience? One of the military masters of the ages was Sun-Tzu, an ancient Chinese teacher and military leader, who lived over two thousand years ago. In many ways his teachings might be appropriate for any contemporary head coach.

> *He who knows the enemy and himself, will never in a hundred battles be at risk.*
> *He who does not know the enemy but knows himself, will sometimes win and sometimes lose.*
> *He who knows neither the enemy nor himself, will be at risk in every battle.*
>
> ***Sun-Tzu***
> ***Chinese Military Leader***

If he lived in the present day, it is safe to say that Sun-Tzu would be an advocate of advance scouting and the study of films of the opposing team. In his teachings, he stressed knowledge over brute force, and the strategy of gathering as much information as possible about the enemy before the battle. In sports, in war, and in investing, history can be invaluable when it comes to giving us information regarding probabilities and tendencies. History is important to every golfer who mentally replays the way that he approached a specific hole the last time on that course. It is important to every manager who reviews the "book" on the tendencies of the opposing pitcher. History is also important to every investor who uses money flow or supply-demand analysis to prepare for the probability of a specific move in the market.

* * *

Let me tell you about a real ballplayer. Over a twenty-year career in the major leagues, he hit 135 home runs, which equals an average of about seven per year. He actually had 9,315 official at-bats, so 135 career home runs means he hit an average of only one home run out of every 101 official at bats. Not very impressive, considering that a modern day power hitter like Sammy Sosa hits one home run out of about every ten or eleven official at-bats.

There's obviously more to his story. Tony Gwynn ended his career with 3,141 hits, and a lifetime batting average of .338, placing him in the top twenty "modern era" players in both categories. But the most amazing stat of all is that 93% of his hits were singles and doubles. Yes, 93%. The baseball Hall of Fame is already waiting for him, and he was just a guy who hit singles and doubles.

Gwynn had a disciplined approach that focused on contact hitting and taking the ball to the opposite field. With an unmatched commitment to time in the cage and time in the viewing room, he exemplified discipline with a capital "D," and he remains a terrific example to those of us who are committed to becoming more successful at this sport we call stock market investing.

As you think about some of the great athletes and coaches that you admire most, begin to focus on their levels of discipline. Many times we can almost see it in their eyes, as our favorite competitors actually take their natural abilities up to another level through practice, preparation, and mental state manipulation. We will continue to explore the ways that mental training and discipline, as well as the other character traits of great sports figures, can help you dial up your "A" game. It can happen. Let the games begin.

CHAPTER TWO:
CONFIDENCE

If one advances confidently in the direction of his dreams, and endeavors to live the life which he has imagined, he will meet with a success unexpected in common hours.

Henry David Thoreau
Author

He wanted to be a big league ballplayer from the start, and that meant wearing heavy catchers gear from his early days in little league. His high school baseball career was full of successes, but the 1988 baseball draft was bittersweet. Yes, he was a draft pick of a great West Coast organization. The problem was that he was picked in the sixty-second round. Of all the numbers in sports, one of the truly amazing ones is 1,389, because that number of prospective players were drafted in 1988 ahead of Mike Piazza—1,389. How hard it must have been for a proud young athlete to keep his confidence in check after a mixed blessing like that. Nevertheless, after that suspect beginning, Piazza obviously has gone on to become an all-star, an elite hitter, and a great example of the power of perseverance and confidence.

Our commitment to any serious endeavor in life is often directly linked to the confidence that we develop in our early experiences with it. The problem is that most other things in life, great or small, are hard before they become easy. Think about the first time you tried to dive off a the high board at the municipal pool. Not easy. Think about the first time you tried to hit a curveball. Not easy. Think about the first time you tried to drive a four-speed. Not easy. Over time you developed confidence to tackle most of life's challenges. It is simple to say, but everything in life is hard before it is easy. If you do something well in life somewhere along the way you built a wall of confidence, brick by brick, and trial by trial. This invisible wall strengthened over time and gave you the confidence to take on more of life's challenges.

In much the same way, the world's great athletes weren't born with protective pads to shield them from hits to their self-confidence. They started small, and built protective barriers that lesser athletes were never quite able to create. All-star, all-pro athletes are a pleasure to watch when a game is on the line because everything seems to slow down around them. The clutch players see everything just a little sooner and a little clearer than the other guys on the court, or on the field. Jordan in the final seconds. Gretzky in overtime. Marino in the final two minutes. Jeter in the last at bat.

If you really want to become a serious investor, then you should start right now to build your own wall of self-confidence. It's good to take your time and build it right, so that after it's built it can withstand opposing shots that one brick alone would never be able to handle.

Courage is largely habit and self-confidence.

General George S. Patton
Allied Forces General WWII

* * *

Jimmie Johnson coached the Dallas Cowboys to a record of one victory and fifteen losses during the 1989 season. Four short years later, in 1993, his Cowboys won it all, Super Bowl XXVII.

In the 1984 NHL draft, 116 hockey players were drafted ahead of Brett Hull. Nevertheless, Hull has gone on to become one of the best offensive players ever to hit the ice.

Midway through the 1951 season, his first in the big leagues, Mickey Mantle was sent back down to the minor leagues, not because of injury, but because of poor performance. This seems almost unthinkable for those of us who include "the Mick" in debates about that elite short list of the best to ever play the game.

Guys like Jimmie Johnson, Brett Hull, and Mickey Mantle certainly had different personalities, but they all exemplified a special breed of sportsmen who had a controlled level of self-confidence that carried them along the roller coaster ride known as a professional sports career. All of the great and not-so-great coaches and athletes ride the roller coaster. While some develop the inner confidence to deal with it, many more never quite get it. Anyone, player or coach, who even gets to the professional level in his sport has an obvious level of raw talent, but the distinctly great ones have a distinctly great level of inner confidence.

> *You need to play with supreme confidence or else you'll lose again, and then losing becomes a habit.*
>
> ***Joe Paterno***
> ***Legendary College Football Coach***

In stock market investing, the masters who make it to the top often possess the self-confidence of Jack, or Arnie, or Tiger. Successful investors share a special confidence and a special trust in their instincts that helps smooth out the peaks and valleys of the investing experience. Although generally street smart and logical, the trait that often gets great investors over the top is a supreme level of confidence in a supreme system. While there is no perfect scientific equation that always works, almost all successful investors have some kind of "system." (We discuss specific systems in sections Two and Three.) The development of a system leads to the development of confidence, which leads to improvement in the system, which leads to more confidence, and so on as the cycle continues. Never to be taken lightly, a defined system of investing is often a key ingredient in the recipe of success for the confident investor.

Stop . . . somewhere along the journey you must differentiate between confidence and blind ego. Don't take this distinction lightly, because it may be as important to your ultimate success as anything else in the game. Controlled confidence is a powerful ally, and it is great to have it on the sideline with you. Blind, uncontrolled ego is not your ally, and can actually become your worst enemy. As you increase your positive feel for your investing system, it's fine to dial up higher levels of self-confidence, as long as you don't allow yourself to go past the red line into the "blind ego" zone.

Why? The reason is that, in the land of investing, the opposition is never going to make it easy for you. In this land, the opponent is not just some defensive lineman. You see, your opponent is actually the market itself, which at any one moment represents thousands upon thousands of variables and opinions regarding the current fundamental value of stocks. Since no one investor can control these variables that make up the market, you must start the investing process by controlling your own ego. If you fail to keep your ego in check, it can pull you down like a ball and chain. The Wall Street ocean bottom is littered with stories of vain, ego-driven stock traders who drowned in the sea of market forces because they were foolish enough to think that they could control something about the market.

Work hard on making the distinction between blind ego and controlled confidence. Strong confidence to fight the force of the waves is great, but blind ego that leaves you exposed to the undertow of the ocean is not. The savvy, streetsmart investor realizes that he is never going to be stronger or smarter than the market. Does the market have a brain? No. Then how can you outsmart something that has no brain? Now that's something to think about.

The year was . . .?

The first night baseball game is played at Wrigley Field

Dell Computer goes public

Michael Douglas wins Best Actor Award for his role in

"Wall Street"

Lakers defeat Pistons for NBA Championship

Randy Johnson makes $70,000 in his first season with the Montreal Expo's

Dow Jones Industrial Average closes the year at 2,169

The year was . . . 1988.

Step back. Let's look at sports from the perspective of a "statistician" for a minute. In the end, a game of sport is a succession of trials that gives a player an opportunity to succeed or fail multiple times during the game. Fans view these multiple trials as "points" in tennis, "plays" in football, and "possessions" in hockey. They actually unfold as mini-games within a game. The odds of being successful in any one sports trial are often relatively low. You have to look no further than basketball or baseball to find examples of trials that exhibit failure more than half of the time.

The average field goal percentage in the NBA in 2001 was 41%. Thousands of two-pointers, three-pointers, and slams woven togther during the season resulted in a success ratio of only four in ten. In many of life's activities, 41% might be viewed as a lousy success ratio, but not so in the NBA. Great contemporary basketball players such as Kobe Bryant, Alan Iverson, and Tim Duncan prove that you can be an all-star in the NBA, make millions of dollars a year, and still fail at your field-goal trials almost 60% of the time.

What a great way to live your life. That's the point. Life is not about perfection. Sure, it's about winning some of the trials, but mostly its about developing your talent so that you stay in the games, get lots of trials, and give your successes a chance to overcome your failures.

Over an extended career, a guy who hits over .330 in the major leagues is a lock to be nominated for induction into the Major League Baseball Hall of Fame. The record shows that in the era of modern baseball (post 1909), only twenty-five players have career batting averages above .330. Names like Ruth, Gehrig, Cobb, and Williams jump out at you. These elite guys are widely recognized as baseball's best, yet they still failed in their hitting trials somewhere around 65% of the time. They failed at this rate in game after game after game, year after year after year, over careers that in many cases spanned twenty years or more.

You see, the great ones have a special mindset, a gift that centers on the idea that: "Failure is a good thing, because it simply gets me closer to success. Failure is okay, because it gets me closer to another trial, which ultimately gets me closer to success." That resilient, confident mindset gives successful athletes the potential to be one of the most successful groups of stock investors in the world. Like bamboo, their approach is one of bend, but don't break. Even the athletes we admire the most lead lives full of failure, success, and failure, until somewhere along the way it all comes together for them.

Think about something important that you do every week in your business or your personal life. Now think what it would be like if you were only successful at it 35% of the time. Could you deal with that? The ability of a great athlete or coach to filter failure from success is an amazing positive.

In team sports, a player often is forced to make a split-second decision and response based upon an incomplete set of information. Consider the quarterback who is forced to react to a moving defensive set. Think about the hockey goalie who must react to power play pressure in a fraction of a second. Scientists estimate that a hitter must react to a big league fastball within four-tenths of one second from the time it is released by the pitcher. It's no wonder that the probability of any player being a success, and ultimately a winner, depends upon so many variables that he can't control. But the constant that all great athletes seem to control is a superior level of confidence—confidence in their abilities, in their instincts, and in their system.

Just as the roster of a professional sports team is comprised of veterans and rookies, the roster in the world of investing is made up of seasoned veterans and unseasoned rookies. That's just the way it is. In order to easily differentiate the rookie approach from the veteran approach going forward, we will identify the less sophisticated, less disciplined investors as RSIs (rookie stock investors), and the more sophisticated, more disciplined investors as VSIs (veteran stock investors).

Both RSIs and VSIs can learn a lot about confidence from great athletes, because an athlete simply has no time to dwell on the concept of perfection. Amazingly, the confidence of the great athlete is founded on the belief, deep down in the gut, that the ultimate end result of failure is success. For them, failure is just a seed that leads to the harvest of some future success. Much like dry seasons are followed by rainy seasons, which are followed by dry seasons, failure is simply a part of the "failure-success-failure" process. Failure is no big deal. It is just one of the outcomes in the process.

The best VSIs (veteran stock investors) that I have had the pleasure to know and study are quietly confident. They often avoid the attention and bright lights of the "star system," and they don't need daily ego enhancement shots. Somewhere along the way these veterans figured out that they don't have to be number one on the performance charts. Sure, they strive to rank consistently high when compared to their peers. Often times this reliability makes them similar to an NFL team that makes the playoffs almost every year. You know what I'm talking about. Remember the Steelers of the eighties, or the Forty-niners of the nineties. These were superior franchises over extended periods of time, and they prove that if you strive for consistency of performance, you sometimes make it all the way to the Super Bowl. Great franchises honored in recent years, like the Lakers, Rams, and Redwings, prove that "consistency" may be a better goal than "perfection." The lesson here is a strong one, and should not be taken lightly. As a stock investor, if your confidence just allows you to "make the playoffs" every year, you can be amazingly successful over a long career in the market.

Unfortunately, I have also worked with clients who have allowed ego and uncontrolled confidence to interfere with their ability to make sound business decisions. One client who comes to mind shall be named Mr. G. He always had to buy recognizable, newsworthy companies so that he could talk about them at work and at the golf course. The performance of his portfolio suffered during the weak market in 2000 and 2001 because he was simply not capable of admitting failure. He would never take defensive action when the signals of the market warranted it. With him, it was definitely an ego thing, and his ego would not allow him to sell a stock that he had just hyped to his golfing buddies. Unbridled ego clouded his ability to accept the failure-success-failure concept, and he suffered greatly because of it.

Like a temperature control thermostat in an office building full of computers, you should strive to increase your investor confidence and keep it at a high but consistent level that is never too high and never too low. Anything you do to work toward higher lows and lower highs will reward you over time, because controlled confidence is a great compnion. If your personal thermostat keeps you comfortable with the controlled realization that "things are rarely as good or as bad as they seem," then you're getting there. Why? Because with time, distance, and the proper perspective, things rarely are as good or as bad as they seem.

Take your lead from quietly confident athletes of this era like Kurt Warner, Tim Duncan, and Derek Jeter. They are some of the best of the breed, but we would enjoy the opportunity to have dinner or hang out with any one of them. By emulating the quiet confidence of guys like Warner, Duncan, and Jeter, we can all start to develop the confident mindset of a true winner. As we do so, we can grow as members in that elite club made up of guys who would not hesitate to say the following:

> "Striking out does not diminish me as a person;
> Giving up an interception does not diminish me as a person;
> Making a bad investment decision does not diminish me as a person;
> Hitting a tee shot into the woods does not diminish me as a person;
> Missing a shot at the buzzer does not diminish me as a person; or

Taking a loss on a stock does not diminish me as a person. One failure does not diminish me as a person; but it does get me one step closer to the next success."

Quiet confidence—a great companion.

CHAPTER THREE:
FOCUS

There are but two powers in the world, the sword and the mind. In the long run, the sword is always beaten by the mind.

Napoleon
Military Leader

Over the course of a full baseball season, the average major league ballplayer gets around 500 official at-bats. The average player strikes out between seventy-five and 100 times, or roughly 15% to 20% of the time. Remember that these guys are the best in the world at what they do, and that, for the professional hitter, a strikeout is not only failure, it is total failure. It means that he did not even put the ball in play. It means that he gave himself no chance for a successful outcome. If the fact that the average professional player fails totally by striking out over 15% of the time seems like a significant number of failures to you, that is understandable. That's just the way it is for even the best in the business of professional baseball.

Nevertheless, in one special year several decades ago, one career legend had a career year. That year in 456 official at-bats, he struck out only twenty-seven times. That's a ratio of less than 6%.

How do you define focus? When baseball historians think about focus, this player is often at the top of the list. Focus on the next pitch in the game meant everything to this hitter. To him focus started in spring training each year with a study of opposing pitchers and their tendencies. It meant having the patience to wait for a truly good pitch, seeking to make contact, and letting the baseball gods take it from there. In that special season, he actually had more home runs than strike-outs, thirty-seven homers to twenty-seven strike-outs. Along the way, his tremendous focus and mindset also led him to a season batting average of .406, making him the last player to beat the magic .400 mark. You know by now that his name was Ted Williams, and the year was 1941.

He simply wanted to be known as the best, not just in Boston, but in all of baseball, and he was arguably that (at least from the left side of the plate). Ted Williams had focus and mental toughness, and an attitude in a time before the media reported on players having an "attitude."

In the tradition of Ted Williams, we are blessed to see today's great athletes consistently dial up high levels of mental focus so often on the late night sports highlights that we sometimes take them for granted. We watch a great tour professional like Phil Mickelson shut out the fact that millions of spectators and television viewers are watching him. We watch a great NBA player, like Kobe Bryant, totally focus on the shot, rather than the fanatical opposing fans. Love 'em or hate 'em, guys like these are a pleasure to watch.

It is a mistake to look too far ahead. Only one link in the chain of destiny can be handled at a time.

Winston Churchill
Statesman, British Prime Minister

Following the wisdom of Churchhill, the great ones in sports develop an unmatched level of mental focus by handling only one link in the chain of destiny at a time. Like a complex water filtration system that filters out impurities, they have an inner ability to simplify all the whirling elements of the sports situation that surrounds them. "Showtime" is time to dial it up a notch. In high stakes game situations, supreme athletes often seem to move well beyond a mental "comfort zone" into that realm that modern sports psychologists now call "the zone."

Superior athletes have a level of focus that makes us proud to be sports fans. On game day we can almost hear the great ones say stuff like: "This is a big game because it's the only game that I can help win today." This is a big situation because it is the only "link in the chain of destiny" that I have some control over today.

The best veteran stock investors (VSIs) that I have had the pleasure to know and study have a similar type of focus. They shut out the noise of extraneous events that they have no control over, they simplify their stroke, and they stay focused on the next pitch that life is going to throw at them. Successful investors in the market don't worry obsessively about the actions of the herd. Their attention is not on the actions of the masses, nor on the sensationalism that the media often creates. It is on their own individual responses and their own personal reflexes.

Do not let what you can't do interfere with what you can do.

John Wooden

Legendary College Basketball Coach

VSIs realize that the financial media will not be accountable to them in the future. What's the point? Do you really think that some guest media personality is going to contact you a year from now to see how his market predictions and forecasts were able to help you? I doubt it. The great ones in the field of stock market investing have an independent approach grounded by the concept that no single analyst (or investor) can actually control much about the market. Like a great hitter reads a pitch as it is released, great stock investors read the market situation, and then react to it. The great ones have a level of focus that allows them to keep their emotions in check, because they are not chasing things that they cannot control. In the words of John Wooden, they "do not let what they can't do interfere with what they can do." As a result, they experience lower highs and higher lows than the average guy. They operate like a car that can't go over seventy or under fifty, so the investing experience is smoother and steadier for them than it is for untested rookies.

Great investors are not necessarily 100% focused from their first day in the markets. In most cases they pay their dues, like college tuition, with real money, real time and real emotion. Like the experience of August two-a-day football drills for the college player, real experience and real financial sweat is mandatory. You can read all the books you want to about successful investing, but until you invest in the real world markets in real time with real money, you will never truly know what it is like to live the life of a sharp successful investor.

Why is it that brilliant mathematicians, who write books about how to be successful playing draw poker, continue to write books? They should all be self-sufficient professional gamblers. Since they're not, the reason may be that there is a "disconnect" between being an expert regarding poker probability tables, and really experiencing the game with a serious amount of your own money on the line. Widely diverse human variables and emotions affect the outcome of a poker game in ways that sometimes overpower the standard mathematical chances of winning or losing. Consider these tough questions. What is the look on the face of the guy at the table with the best cards? What is the look on the face of the player with the worst cards? Which player bets first? Which player draws the most cards? Which player just drew to an inside straight, and what body language did he exhibit at that moment? How can you answer these questions by reading a book? Maybe you can't. That's the point.

The year was . . .?

George Brett becomes the 18th player in history to get 3000 hits
America Online goes public
Redskins defeat Bills in Super Bowl
Blue Jays win the World Series over the Braves
Pittsburgh defeats Chicago for the Stanley Cup
Dow Jones Industrial Average closes the year at 3,301

The year was . . . 1992.

It is often the tough, gut-wrenching decisions that actually teach us the most, because nothing can compare to having real money exposed to real market risk. Before there was reality TV, there was the school of hard knocks, which helped today's best investors find focus in an approach that seems to say, "I can't control what the market is doing, so my best option is to stay mentally tough and control the way that I respond to whatever the market throws at me." Sure, sometimes decisions are made that look as bad as a quarterback sack. But the best investors and money managers have an ability to quickly jump back up after a bad play, adjust the gear, and return to the huddle for the next chance at a winning play.

"Regret" does not exist in the vocabulary of the legends, whether in sports or in the stock market, because they are focused on the "now." If you don't believe that, look at a close-up of the eyes of one of your favorite athletes when he is on the field of battle. The eyes of the great players show that they have already deleted the last bad play from their memory banks. Their controlled concentration simplifies and smooths out the sporting process into one of consistently lower highs and higher lows.

Attaining lofty levels of mental focus is not easy, but it can be done. The good news is that when you get to a superior level of mental focus, you can stay there for a long time, hopefully for the rest of your life. Coincidentally, legendary running backs Jim Brown, Earl Campbell, and Terrell Davis all retired from the game of football at the age of thirty. It is common knowledge that the average playing career in the NFL is less than five years, and almost all great athletes face some physical limitations as they get into their late thirties and forties. But the stock market creates its own league. Assuming that your mind stays sharp, there is no reason that you can't have an investing career that spans many decades.

* * *

Early in his college career, five guys were ahead of him on the quarterback depth chart. Never considered a first round draft pick, he was actually the 82nd overall pick in the 1979 NFL draft. He didn't fit the stereotype of the big, strong quarterback. However, in the reality test known as game situations, he became known as one of the best clutch, come-from-behind quarterbacks in football history. In key pressure situations, he had an unmatched level of focus and mental toughness. John Madden once described him as the best offensive player that he had ever seen. He is the only player who was named Super Bowl Most Valuable Player three times, and he led the NFL in passing five times in the decade of the eighties (1981 to 1990). Joe Montana played with focus and finesse, and he is highly regarded as one of the finest offensive football players of the twentieth century.

In the stock market, and in life, success often comes to those who develope the instincts of a two-minute-drill quarterback like Joe Montana. VSIs, like veteran quarterbacks, focus on what they see at that moment. They read the tone of the market like a great quarterback reads an opposing defensive set, and they focus on what the market indicators are saying to them on that particular day. Because they have confidence in the long-term rewards of capitalism and the free market system, big league investors are not interested in trying to predict exactly where the S&P 500 Equity Index will be at some point a few months or years in the future. They leave that to the TV talking heads with the stadium-sized egos. Anyone can make predictions regarding who will make the NBA Championship finals next year, or the year after that. The question becomes, can anyone actually make these predictions with accuracy and consistency over an extended period of time? No. So let the market forecasters do their thing, but always keep the proper perspective. Rather than fumbling with the future, focus on strategies to help you interpret what the market is trying to tell you, at this moment, right now, today.

The main thing is to keep the main thing the main thing.

Stephen Covey

Author, Motivational Speaker

Stephen Covey's quote sounds almost too simple, doesn't it? The fact is that we can all find a lot of common sense and wisdom in these words, which remind us to focus on the moment, focus on the facts, and focus on the next opportunity that life is about to give us.

In later chapters, we will explore the amazingly positive history of our free enterprise system, and the foundation of confidence that it has created for all of us. That foundation allows the masters in the market to focus almost completely on reading and monitoring the opposing information of the market. VSIs are able to read the current market situation like a PGA tournament player reads a putting surface, knowing that no two are exactly alike.

Like expert craftsman, stock market investors can attain similar levels of consistency and focus. Most RSIs (rookie stock investors) don't focus properly on the present because they either have "regrets" about their past trading mistakes, or they have "fear" of failure with their current market holdings. They don't get a grip on the simple fact that history is now only a highlight video. While we should all learn from our mistakes, regret adds no value for the healthy investor. Events that happened one trade ago, or one play ago, are gone and can never be recaptured.

Nothing is as far away as one minute ago.

Jim Bishop
Author, Columnist

Great athletes have already put yesterday behind them, and that ability to "focus without regret" is one of the great character traits of professional athletes that helps elevate them in the eyes of the serious sports fan. Imagine for a minute a top professional pitcher, like Pedro Martinez, who starts a game with optimism and adrenaline, only to have the leadoff batter hit a home run. High hopes are bruised, and now any chance of a no-hitter is gone. Any chance of a shutout is gone. What would the best of the best do? A pitcher like Pedro

Martinez would regroup mentally, focus on the next pitch, and focus on some other outcome such as winning the game. All true sports fans have seen this kind of thing happen at the professional level in the form of the great comeback, or the two-minute drill, or the walk-off home run.

> *Get mad, then get over it.*
>
> **Colin Powell**
> ***U.S. Secretary of State***

"Get over it." This is not to say that we should never plan for the future. Even though VSI's can't forecast the future any better than the rest of us, the vision of the most successful market investors includes intermediate and long-term plans of how they want to improve their quality of life. They approach life and investing a lot like they would approach a long road trip across the country, one short leg at a time. On a road journey from San Diego to Boston, you don't know what the weather or road conditions will be like 500 miles down the highway, but that doesn't stop you from taking the trip. If you focus on the present, and getting your vehicle safely through the next 500 yards, you eventually make progress over the next 500 miles. You don't drive the same speed all the time, in the market or in anything else in life. You respect road hazards and detours, and the important thing is that you stay focused and attentive so that you can make headway safely without major setbacks.

In many ways, it is reasonable to compare your investing journey to a road journey from San Diego to Boston. Even if you have prepared well for the trip, you have to maintain focus over every mile, one mile at a time. Uncertainty is a part of the process of traveling, but because you know you have to make progress, you place focus over fear of the unknown.

As amazing as the brain is, any human mind has a limited capacity to process and filter information. If a great old stadium like Lambeau Field is filled to capacity, it's filled to capacity. If your mind is overcome with fear, where are you going to find the mental capacity to process other new information in a calm, logical manner? You aren't. If you suppress the fear of the unknown that occupies valuable space between your ears, you increase your ability to focus on information that may benefit you right now.

Don't let fear of some unknown market monster take up space and get in the way of your focus on the present conditions in the market. In your emotional depth-chart, focus should always occupy one of the top slots on the list. I sincerely believe that great athletes focus on the present moment as well as any other class of people in the world. Emulate them in your approach to the markets by leaving fear and regret in the locker room every time you step out into daylight.

Since most master investors have their priorities in order, they have attained a certain level of understanding that includes the idea that it is much more important to make money than it is to be right. Wait a minute. Being right is not important? That's right. You got it.

The great VSIs know that one bad investment decision is just like "one play in one game in the football season of life," and that being right is overrated. Making money is the only scoreboard that counts. The money masters know that the free enterprise system will offer them a reasonably high probability of success in the long run, if they just stick to their playbook. To them, small setbacks are just a part of the game, like a bad call or a slow field. Jabs and stomach punches are no big deal, as long as you never let one punch take you out.

* * *

He grew up in Mobile, Alabama, the son of a steel worker. He lacked good fundamental coaching in his early years as a baseball player, and as a result he actually learned to bat cross-handed. For a right-handed hitter, that meant that he held the bat with his left hand above his right hand. The style was awkward, but the strength came. In the long run, that cross-handed style probably strengthened his wrists as much as anything he could have done.

His historic major league career was one of focus and consistency. Although he never had any Maris or McGwire years of sixty-plus homeruns, over one historic span of nineteen years (1955-1973), he averaged thirty-five homers per season. Even though he received death threats as he approached Babe Ruth's standing record of 714 home runs, the end of the story is that Hank Aaron had the focus to break the Babe's record, and then some. He ended his career with 755 home runs, a record that obviously still stands. He also got 3,771 hits, and batted .305 over his career, and further proof that he was a "complete" player is shown by the fact that he was the first player in baseball history to hit over 500 home runs and collect over 3,000 hits. You don't put up numbers like that unless you have the focus of a fighter pilot. Sure, Hank Aaron had God-given ability and desire, but he also had a level of focus that was as good as it gets.

CHAPTER FOUR:
FLEXIBILITY

When you come to a fork in the road, take it.

Yogi Berra
Philosopher, Baseball Legend

* * *

To many experts, home team advantage in the NFL is a huge positive. Call it the "twelfth-man syndrome" or something. In 1998, the Denver Broncos were an AFC Wildcard team, which meant that they went on the road to play in all three of their playoff games. They won all three, on their way to the championship victory over Green Bay in Super Bowl XXXII. Call them well coached, or flexible, or both.

He didn't even pay a lot of attention to basketball until he failed to make his high school football team. Now, forty years later, Coach Mike Kryzewski of Duke University is on the short list of the greatest basketball minds to ever step on a college court. He is making his mark, not in his boyhood dream of football, but on a basketball court.

In his first six seasons in the majors, he had a very mediocre pitching record of thirty-six wins and forty losses. Was he out of his league, or was he a late bloomer? You decide. He was flexible enough to change some things about his mechanics and his control, and he went on to a record of ninety-seven wins and twenty-seven losses in his final four seasons. That's a 78% success ratio, remarkable for any pitcher of any era. Even though an arthritic arm forced him to retire well before his time, Sandy Koufax (Los Angeles Dodgers) became the youngest man ever to be inducted into the Hall of Fame.

* * *

Remember when you were a kid, and you played all kinds of sports in the neighborhood or at recess? With a little practice, you became pretty good at pickup basketball, touch football, street baseball, and maybe even roller hockey. If your team needed a pitcher, you tried pitching. If your team needed a pass-rusher, you were the man (boy). If your team needed a goalie for a game or two, you played goalie. You may not have been the most talented kid on the block, but you had flexibility.

As you continued to play organized sports, the system probably forced you to specialize more and more as you got older. If you played high school football, chances are you did not play both offense and defense. You may have been on the swim team, or the track team, or the golf team, but it's doubtful that you played on more than one of them unless you attended a very small high school. The athletic systems in place were simply too specialized, so the instinctive flexibility that you had as a child athlete in the neighborhood games diminished. That's simply the way it worked out for most of us.

* * *

He has a unique place in the record books because he is one of only two NFL head coaches to win at least three Super Bowls. One of the most amazing facts about his professional coaching career is that he won three different Super Bowls with three different quarterbacks. Joe Gibbs, of the Washington Redskins, was a head coach who constantly evolved in order to get the most out of his various lineups. In a world where so many people slip into a comfort zone, it is refreshing to study a great man who found success by adapting to change. All football fans recognize the critical importance of the quarterback as the offensive leader of the team. In contrast to a fine coach like Chuck

Noll, who had Terry Bradshaw lead his offense in all four of his championships, Joe Gibbs won three Super Bowls with three distinctly different quarterbacks.

Joe Theissman, while athletically talented, was also a great thinker. Mark Rypien had a rocket launcher for an arm. Then there was Doug Williams, a scrambler who may have had more athletic talent than either of the other two. In the end, Joe Gibbs found success with each of the three distinct styles. That's flexibility. In the case of Joe Gibbs, his flexibility as a head coach was exemplified by his ability to take any specific mix of players, and then evolve with the game by developing strategies that played to the strengths of those players. That instinctively flexible approach led Joe Gibbs to an exceptional coaching career with the Redskins during the eighties and early nineties, a period when the National Football League was evolving into greatness.

Devise your strategy according to the changing posture of the enemy to determine the course and outcome of the battle.

Sun-Tzu
Chinese Military Leader

Like great coaches and athletes, VSIs (veteran stock investors) have a more flexible approach to their job than the average guy on the street. They often have no desire to be predictable. Somewhere along the way they figured out that even though flexibility and adaptability do not guarantee success, those qualities can keep you in the game. When things get tough, a flexible approach can help you see a negative situation from a fresh perspective, and that can make all the difference. In the real world, anybody who is a success would probably admit that he suffered defeats and setbacks, changed a few things, and tried again. Every professional was at some point an amateur who did not quit.

I will find a way, or I will make a way.

anonymous

Think of the most successful coaches, teachers, and businessmen that you have had the privilege of knowing. They probably viewed problems as temporary rather than permanent. They knew that positive results often come to athletes and investors who don't crumble when things go wrong, and they believed in their hearts that success can come to those who are flexible enough to try a different approach, or a different angle.

Coaches like Joe Gibbs had an instinctive, natural understanding of the basic concepts found in *"Who Moved My Cheese,"* by Spencer Johnson, M.D. This wonderfully simple parable spells out several themes about "change," including it will happen, anticipate it, monitor it, adapt to it, and enjoy it. Isn't that what makes life, and sport, so interesting? New challenges. New obstacles. New opponents. New schedules. New possibilities. New potential conquests.

The history of the stock market is full of great examples of how change, either real or perceived, can dramatically alter the value of a share of common stock. Coca-Cola stock provides an illustration of how a great company's stock can fluctuate wildly, even if the nature of the underlying company does not. In a period from 1995 through 1998, when the Coca-Cola Company was one of the darlings of Wall Street, it often traded as high as fifty to sixty times current earnings per share. In 1998, it actually traded as high as $88 per share, but as sentiment and market conditions eroded over the next two years, Coca-cola traded down to $48 per share. Did Coca-Cola, the company, dramatically change the way it did business during that period of time? Not really, yet the value of the common stock fell by 45%, simply because of changes in the public's perceived value of the company.

* * *

Back in the sixties, I had the privilege to play high school athletics with a young man who lacked the use of his right arm from the elbow down. He was not born that way, but a car accident when he was just a young boy left him with the problem. His name was Eddie D. Did he give up participating in sports because of his problem? Not exactly. Much like Jim Abbott, (Major League pitcher, 1989-1999, California Angels, New York Yankees), he compensated for his handicap by working with it, not against it.

Eddie D. developed an uncanny ability to chase down fly balls in the outfield, make one-handed catches with his glove hand, flip the ball and the glove into the air in one motion, catch the ball in mid-air, and throw it into the infield. All this action was accomplished in practically the same length of time that it took any other player to make that play. As a hitter, by using his right arm mostly to balance the bat, he developed great strength in his left arm, and by so doing became a fine contact hitter as well as a skilled bunter.

Eddie D. was innovative and flexible in his approach. In the end, he probably had more fun with sports than most of the rest of us. Handicap? What handicap?

> *One of the major factors in successful leadership is the willingness to concede a miscalculation or mistake and change course immediately.*
>
> **Bill Walsh,**
> **Former NFL coach, San Francisco Forty-niners**

In stock market investing, history never repeats itself in exactly the same way. Economic trends and financial forces can never be fully forecasted based upon textbook formulas, analysis, or research. RSIs (rookie stock investors) often learn the hard way that the best-laid short-term plans can go "out the window" because of some event or trend that was not properly predicted.

Nevertheless, over long windows of time, stocks, representing the equity ownership in large U.S. companies, have outperformed other asset classes such as treasury bonds, corporate bonds, and treasury bills. While there is comfort in that fact, the reality is that political, economic, and social events have historically created greater volatility in stock values than in bonds and treasury bills. This statistical fact, as much as any other, brings us back to the constant need for the prudent stock investor to monitor, adapt, monitor, and adapt again.

The year was . . .?

> **ESPN (Entertainment and Sports Programming Network) airs for first time**
> **Michigan State defeats Indiana State for NCAA basketball title.**
> **Pirates over Orioles in World Series**
> **Lee Iococca becomes C.E.O. of Chrysler Corporation**
> **Steelers defeat Cowboys in the Super Bowl**
> **Dow Jones Industrial Average closes out year at 839**

The year was . . . 1979.

Think about some of the major events of your lifetime, such as the assassination of President John Kennedy, the fall of the Berlin Wall, Iraq's invasion of Kuwait, and the World Trade Center terrorist attack. The list gets longer when you include less sensational events such as interest rate changes, expansions, recessions, and government policy changes. The global uncertainty of the twenty-first century makes it mandatory that you, as an investor, remain flexible in your approach to the markets. You must be like the skilled defensive end that shifts his approach depending on the size and strength and force of the opponent. You must never marry yourself to one stance regarding the direction of the market. You must be willing and able to shift your perspective with the flow of market trends with no hesitation. Since you cannot control the forces of the market, you must control your perspective and your actions. Since you cannot control the rules of the game, you must control how you respond to the rules of the game. Sometimes that means pulling the trigger and taking an action that may have seemed totally unreasonable just a few days earlier.

What about the experts that say you should just "buy and hold" by purchasing a basket of stocks and holding that fixed portfolio without ever changing it? In the new world of the 2000s, a passive buy and hold approach is less than prudent, and may prove to be very hazardous to the health of your portfolio. Many highly successful money managers and professional investors prefer an active, flexible, approach. The reasons for this perspective primarily have to do with the effects of emotion and investor psychology. If you prefer to remain rigid and inflexible as an investor, you may make out all right for a while. But what if you take on large paper losses, and then get emotionally squeezed out of the market at the wrong time because you can't take it anymore? If that happens, you lose—you lose capital, you lose confidence, and you lose out on future market opportunities.

Cisco Systems, one of the fine Internet-related companies of the 1990s, became one of the most widely owned stocks in America, and in 1999 it traded as high as $70 per share. By the end of 2001, it was trading around $15 per share, down over 75% from its former high. Cisco Systems is still regarded by some on Wall Street as a fine company, but it is a charred example of the fact that a good company can become a bad stock investment in certain business and psychological climates. If you try to tell the "buy and hold" investor who bought Cisco at $68 that everything is going to be all right, you won't get very far. Because of inflexibility, market myopia, poor risk management, or all of the above, that investor is stuck with a problem. The fact is, even if Cisco stock improves at an average annual rate of 15% per year in the foreseeable future, it will take the investor in our hypothetical example eleven years just to get back to his entry price of $68 per share.

The New York Stock Exchange and the NASDAQ Exchange give us hundreds of similar examples that kicked investors in the kneecaps over the past few years. Alert: It does not have to be that way, and flexibility in your approach to the market can help you avoid destructive, negative numbers like those described above. Sometimes it all starts with something as simple as being willing to accept things contrary to your current belief system.

As water varies its flow according to the fall of the land, so an army varies its method of gaining victory according to the enemy.

Sun-Tzu

Chinese Military Leader

The events that shape our lives are in many ways like the flow of water, or like the waves on the ocean. All the study and preparation in the world cannot give us the power to totally predict how the forces of the ocean will play out in the future. The tide rises, the tide falls. The ebb and flow of the ocean constantly changes, based upon wind patterns, undercurrents, barometric pressure, and other forces of nature.

Consider the sport of sailing. Think about how difficult sailing is for the novice? He must constantly react to ever-changing weather and physical conditions without trying to overpower them. With experience, the best sailors learn that they cannot control the elements, so they are better off to go with the flow that the elements give them. They can't use force to master the ocean, so they must learn to work in concert with it. Sailors first study the flow of the wind and the currents, and then they set their sails so that they have the greatest opportunity to benefit, and make progress towards their ultimate destination.

Successful VSIs approach the markets with the same logic. They never feel helpless because they know that they possess the intelligence and instincts to react to an ocean of ever-changing events, opinions, and market conditions. The best sailors have an unwavering respect for the ocean. Similarly, the best investors have a high regard for the free market system, and they make progress by taking "measured risks," not blind risks, in an attempt to go with the flow and the force of the market. All-star investors use barometer-like indicators to measure the risk in any market situation relative to the potential reward, and then they adjust their course appropriately. They do this not once or twice, but time after time.

With sailing, mastering the basics is fairly simple, but you still learn something new almost every time you go out. The basics are critically important, but a sailor's knowledge bank grows over time because each excursion is a separate set of events. With experience, the best sailors learn how the hull, the rudder, and the sails interact with the wind and the elements, and how the positive interaction between all of these variables can work together to put the sailing vessel on a more accurate course.

On the water, "change" is simply one of the rules of the game. A sailor can't control the forces of nature, but he can control the set of his sails. A serious investor can't control the forces of supply, demand and emotion, but he can control the set of his perspective and his portfolio.

That's sailing. That's investing. That's flexibility. You are probably familiar with the famous quote of the great Yogi Berra, "when you come to a fork in the road, take it." If you always remain flexible in your approach to the markets, you too can become an investor that even "Yogi" would be proud of.

Now we move on, knowing that discipline, confidence, focus and flexibility are great allies of the serious investor.

What else can we learn from the great coaches and athletes of this or any other era? For starters, how about the following:

A sporting experience (game) is a series of mostly meaningless failures, interrupted by some highly meaningful successes.

An investing experience (game) is a series of mostly meaningless failures, interrupted by some highly meaningful successes.

SECTION TWO:
THE DEFENSE (A MEETING WITH THE DEFENSIVE COORDINATOR)

CHAPTER FIVE:

THE DEFENSIVE FOUNDATION

The expectations of life depend on diligence; the craftsman that would perfect his work must first sharpen his tools.

Confucius
Chinese Philosopher

Think about it. Whenever you were successful at anything in your life, it was probably the result of some mental plan of attack. The plan may have been simple, or it may have been complex, but you probably found success because you first formed some internal vision of success, and then you acted on that vision. The internal vision helped ground you and energize you. As a youngster you may have imagined that you were Joe Montana or Terry Bradshaw in the fourth quarter of the Super Bowl, or maybe you pretended that you were Reggie Jackson or George Brett in the seventh game of the World Series.

As a parent or professional, your plan may have been a particularly positive note or action list that you wrote on your Day-Timer™ and reviewed every day. Maybe more sophisticated techniques like visualization were a part of your mental game plan, but regardless, just as the letter "p" comes before the letter "s" in the alphabet, there's a good chance that the "plan" came before the "success."

When your Dad was teaching you how to drive a car, did he ever bark out the line, "leave yourself an out?" He might have been more specific with instructions like, "don't ever attempt to pass a big rig on a bridge, " or a rule like, "even when the light turns green, be aware of the other cars at the intersection." Sure, you were probably listening at only 50%, but he really was 100% interested in your well-being. Your Dad was simply telling you to always be aware of your personal driving defense, because he knew better than you that defensive, reactive options in the case of some negative event would lessen the odds that you might be involved in a serious accident. This type of fatherly advice in many ways resembles the great anonymous business wisdom, "if you watch the downside, the upside will take care of itself." It's a simple, but effective, rule for success, whether you're on the streets, on the playing fields, or in the markets.

> *The primary challenge of coaching in the NFL is to get people to do what they don't want to do in order to achieve what they want to achieve.*
>
> ***Tom Landry***
> ***Legendary NFL coach***

To some investors it seems boring and negative to think about defense and loss control, but the reality is that most truly successful stock market investors incorporate a disciplined defense in their formula for success. You may not like all this talk about damage control and defense, but experience through some of the most volatile times in the history of the U.S. markets has made me ever mindful of the adage that your "investing defense will always keep you in the game."

Many great investors share something with the head football coaches out there who started their careers as defensive line coaches or defensive coordinators, because they have the highest regard for a sound defense in the total scheme of things. Some of the most respected contemporary head coaches in the NFL, including Bill Belicheck (Patriots), Dave Wannstedt (Dolphins), and Tony Dungy (Colts), all came up through the ranks as defensive coordinators. Consider a legendary head coach like Tom Landry, who coached the Dallas Cowboys during some of their glory years. Landry played defensive back at the University of Texas, and started his coaching career as a defensive coach for the New York Giants, so defensive strategies were in his blood. Over the years he became an expert in the intricacies of the offense and the special teams, and he is credited with the first serious use of the shotgun offense to the NFL, but he never let his guard down when if came to developing strong defensive players and strategies. One of the implications of Landry's above quote is that emphasis on defense is not always easy or pleasant, but he nevertheless made it Job One. Yes, he was an innovator on both sides of the ball, but defensive concepts like the "flex defense," remain a strong part of the Landry legacy.

Would a dedicated defensive coach scrap his game plan just because he lost a few games in a row? No, I don't think so. This type of coach, like a great field general, would stay with the core defensive system that he had confidence in, and the game plan that got him there. He would do this knowing full well that the offense could get hot or cold, but the defense would keep him, and his team, in the game.

In the fraternity of current NFL coaches, Bill Cowher exemplifies another successful head coach who came from the defensive side of the tracks. He was a gutsy, blue-collar type of linebacker and special teams player with the Browns and the Eagles before a knee injury cut his playing career short in 1984. He spent the next seven years as a defensive secondary coach, and a defensive coordinator with the Chiefs and the Browns, before landing the head job with the Steelers in 1992. Let the record show that Cowher knows defense, and during his tenure the Steelers have consistently ranked among the AFC leaders on defense.

In the great game known as stock market investing, a sound defensive game plan should start with a "defined exit strategy." What does that mean? Much like defensive driving, it means leaving yourself an out. It means setting defined percentage limits on the downside dollar exposure of "every" individual stock that you invest in. In street jargon it means, "cutting your losses." If you set defensive downside limits on only some of your positions, that is as ridiculous as sending only half of your defense onto the field. That makes no sense. As amazing as it may seem to the sports fan, most RSIs (rookie stock investors) go into the game without a defined exit strategy. The inherent weakness in this approach becomes clear when they say something as juvenile as, "I'll just see how it goes. I'll probably sell out when I double my money." That type of mindless, myopic thinking leaves the RSI with no defensive plan, and no "out" on the downside, so just like a driver with no "out," he exposes himself to dangerous negative possibilities.

Would you ever buy a new Porsche 911 Turbo and drive it across the country without insuring it against damage or loss? I don't think so. You know that it's wise to insure any prized possession such as a sports car or a home against the possibility of catastrophic loss. That's common sense, and just good business practice. With that in mind, it is totally amazing that most RSIs do not take any action to insure their assets against the risk of significant loss. Like the defense against catastrophic loss that we know as property and casualty insurance, similar contingency coverage should always be a part of your approach to stock investing. Call it covering all the bases if you want to, but make sure that it includes specific defensive strategies designed to limit the risk of catastrophic loss. Watch your backside, and over time, the upside will take care of itself.

> *Some say that it is a socialist idea that making profits is a vice. I consider the real vice to be making losses.*
>
> **Winston Churchill**
> **Statesman, British Prime Minister**

Let's look at the logic supporting a strategic, defensive approach that includes points where you would exit a stock if its price goes against you. For purposes of this discussion, let us assume that we are "bullish" investors, that is, we own long stock positions because we want the value to go up. Recognizing that no one can perfectly forecast future events, any complete and balanced game plan must include defensive contingencies for those instances when a stock you own buckles and rolls over.

If we were to witness a fight between two kids on a playground, each kid would have his own threshold of pain, or that point at which he would say "uncle." Like it or not, a serious investor should go into each investment battle with a point at which he would say "uncle." That's not necessarily good or bad, that's just the way it has to be. Just as your favorite football team has an offense and a defense, a complete investment game plan should include potential sell strategies not only when a stock becomes profitable, but also when it becomes unprofitable.

Let me warn you that this process is psychologically uncomfortable because it goes against human nature to admit that we were wrong. That's one of the primary reasons that playing defense, and selling a stock at a guaranteed loss, is an act that most rookie investors avoid. It is terrifically hard for the RSI to sell at a loss, because of the common view in our society that a loss is a signal of defeat or low self-worth. His instincts tell him to "just wait it out," or "get out when I get back to even." Burdened by a weak plan and a strong ego, the RSI all too often mistakenly concludes that selling at a guaranteed loss is an error, an embarrassment, and an admission of defeat.

The savvy investor, on the other hand, knows that nothing could be further from the truth. A great irony in the investing game is that the winners seem to focus most on how much they can lose on a transaction, while the losers tend to focus on how much they can win. I know this seems backwards and illogical, but let me repeat that winners seem to focus on how much they can lose. Try it on for size. Just like the auto insurance that protects a prized sports car, protecting your assets, and your financial ammunition, for future battles should never be an embarrassment to you. Protecting your cash and your capital is so much more important than protecting your ego that there is no comparison. You would not self-insure a prized sports car that could be smashed up at any moment because of an event that was out of our control, right? Protecting principal through the use of specific, disciplined, risk control techniques seems unexciting, and is a difficult thing for the rookie investor to grab on to. Don't worry, because we'll get there together.

> *Sell what shows you a loss, and keep what shows you a profit.*
>
> **Jesse Livermore**
>
> **Legendary Investor, Early 1900s**

The common adage on Wall Street is "cut your losses, and let your profits run." I would prefer to restate this primary rule in the following way: "Kill your losses and feed your profits," or: "Kill your losers and nurture your winners." If that gets your attention, so be it, but realize that we are not talking about pets or prisoners of war. We are speaking about getting control over profits and losses, the inanimate keys to your financial health and well-being.

> *Kill your losses and feed your profits. Kill your losers, and feed your winners.*
>
> **Neil Rinehart**

Many market strategists believe that it is wise to have a downside exit discipline based on a specific percentage loss point. An example of this defensive strategy is to pull the trigger and sell out of a losing stock if it drops by 10%. In market talk this is known as a "sell-stop" point, an "uncle" point where a previously entered sell-stop order is triggered.

Consider the following example of a defensive strategy based on a hypothetical company that we shall call "North American Sporting Goods." Assume that our ultimate defensive goal is to manage risk and stop the pain of loss at minus 10%. The math shows that if you buy "North American" at $100 per share, and you set a predetermined loss point at 10%, then if the stock dropped to $90, you would take action to sell the stock. That action would be triggered because the stock, for reasons out of your control, drifted 10% below your original cost of $100 per share.

When a decision has to be made, make it. There is no totally right time for anything.

General George S. Patton
Legendary WW II General

The negative chain of events played out like this in our "North American Sporting Goods" example. You own the stock at a cost of $100 per share. The first major move is down sharply, but because you also placed a predetermined sell-stop order, you sell the stock at your "uncle" point and you stop the pain. Your sell-stop order was your insurance policy. The 10% loss you experienced was the deductible you had to bear, and was much better than a catastrophic loss of 40% or 50%. It is tuition in "Stock Market University," and the loss that you agreed to accept when you made the original investment decision. Like the guy who takes Advil™ at the first sign of a problem, you get ahead of the pain. You are out and you are protected. Even if the stock goes down 90% from this point, you will not suffer another nickel. You are still in the game. Nothing was wiped out. In this investment game hypothetical, your offensive team lost possession of the ball, so your defensive team had to take the field. This is just one of many possible outcomes, but you came prepared for it because you had a defensive action plan. You did not second-guess yourself, or feel great emotion, or feel great remorse. You lost a small part of your investment capital, but you kept a significant part of it. Thanks to your defense, which in this case was a pre-defined sell discipline, you dug in and held your field position against an uncertain opponent, mainly the future. Yes, you may have lost that particular stock and that possession of the ball, but your defense kept you in the game.

The year was . . .?

Canadiens over Blackhawks for the Stanley Cup

Intel invents the first microprocessor

French Connection wins Academy Award for best picture

Texas Instruments introduces first pocket calculator (cost, around $150)

Colts beat Cowboys in Super Bowl

Pirates over Orioles in World Series

Dow Jones Industrial Average closes the year at . . . 890

The year was . . . 1971.

Think back to a time in your youth when you experienced physical pain like a burn, or a break, or a cut. You didn't think so at the time, but that pain was a protective, positive thing. We are not talking about a root canal without anesthesia, but the less traumatic pain of some accidental event that forced you to stop whatever you were doing. The pain of a minor burn on your hand when you were a kid might have caused an immediate reaction that protected you from burning your entire arm. The pain of a minor stock loss should be measured from the same positive perspective. If the pain of a limited loss hurts a little, that's okay because you stay sharp, you learn from the experience, and you increase your chances of long-term investment survival. Like a tough, off-season workout that makes your muscles burn, a little investment pain along the way can actually improve your financial condition for the games in your future.

While there is nothing magical about a minus 10% stop-loss point, it is within the range of minus 8% to minus 15% often used by professional investors. A defined loss percentage, plus an Excel™ spreadsheet or even a $10 calculator, can help you identify specific sell-stop price levels for every new investment you make. As a prudent investor, you should enter a defensive sell-stop order in tandem with every offensive buy you make. This is not advanced calculus, but rather simple stock market survival. You buy an asset that is important to you, and you immediately enter a protective stop order as insurance to protect you against catastrophic loss. In effect, you are insured from the moment you drive the sports car off the dealer's lot. This costs you nothing out of pocket except a little time and effort. If your brand new stock investment goes up, you have nothing to worry about, but if it goes down, you're covered from day one. So, once again, you have nothing to worry about.

Let's revisit our specific "North American Sporting Goods" example, assuming that you buy the stock at $100 per share, and then enter an open sell-stop order with the New York Stock Exchange to sell out and kill your loss if the price drops by 10% to a price of $90. What happens if NASG drops by 9% to $91 a share? If the stock only drops to $91, and then rebounds back to $100 or more, nothing happens to your block of stock because the triggering event, which in this case was defined as market transactions at a price of $90 or lower, never took place. You experience some of the bumps that are a normal part of the journey, but you still hold your investment and all of the upside reward possibilities that go with it.

On the other hand, if the market price of NASG drops to $90, then a specific chain of events occurs. When a transaction is completed at $90, that trade is the triggering event that turns your open "sell-stop" order into a "market" order. Your block of NASG stock then moves in line to become a part of the next market transaction. In a free, fluid market for an actively traded stock, there is a high probability that you would sell out at a price very close to the $90 trigger price. However, note that there is no guarantee of the transaction price, and in the rare case where a stock is in a free-fall, it is possible that the next price level following the $90 trigger price could be either slightly or significantly below that price. Like Derek Jeter crossing second base on the front end of a double play, your sell price should be "in the area." That's just the way it works in a free auction market system. The reality of the marketplace is that, although never guaranteed, there is a high probability that you would sell your stock at a price very close to the pre-defined sell-stop price.

With practice and experience, you will develop greater comfort with your overall game plan if you use sell-stop orders religiously. They are the airbags and anti-lock brakes of a sound investment vehicle, and they are a generally accepted method of making sure that your investing defense keeps you on the road, and in the game. These orders are extremely flexible, and can be entered for one day, or for an extended period of time. After a while they will become habit, just like fastening your seatbelt.

> *A man who has committed a mistake and doesn't correct it is committing another mistake.*
>
> **Confucius**
> **Chinese Philosopher**

While sell-stop orders entered at price levels in a range of minus 10% to minus 15% are reasonable for the moderate investor, it may be justified to use different percentage limits in certain markets. In his insightful book, ***How to Make Money in Stocks***, William O'Neill recommends that investors enter protective, sell-stop orders at levels approximately 7% to 8% below their original cost. With this strategy, if you are wrong you are gone, and gone quickly. On the other hand, if the value of your stock goes up, you can raise your stop order safety net, much like a circus attendant would raise a safety net under a high wire act. O'Neill's more aggressive minus 7% to 8% sell level triggers more transactions during periods of market volatility, but this approach also tightens the limit on downside exposure from any one specific stock, and for that reason alone, it may have merit for more experienced investors.

Protective sell-stop orders are damage control in its simplest form because they allow you to take major, unlimited market risk and reduce it to manageable, limited risk. Consider this. What if you were asked to walk a six-inch beam across a forty-foot span between the rooftops of two ten-story buildings? You don't like heights, and in fact you have a very real case of acrophobia. If you lose your balance, there is nothing to protect you from a 100-foot fall, major bodily injury, and most likely death. For most of us this would be defined as a high-risk situation. Now consider one difference in the scenario. Suppose you are asked to walk across the same six-inch beam. It also spans across a distance of forty feet. But this time we change one key variable. This time the beam is "eighteen inches" off the ground, not 100-feet off the ground. Even if you lose your balance and slip off the beam, you will walk away unharmed, with body intact. You will be able to take on another challenge. By changing just one of the variables of the situation, you reduced a major risk to a minor risk; you reduced an unlimited risk to a limited risk. Consistent use of sell-stop orders will do the same thing for you, and that alone is reason enough to make them an indelible part of your defensive game plan.

CHAPTER SIX:
STAYING IN THE GAME

You already know how to do it. What's that? You have experienced the rewards of taking small, defined losses to protect your wallet if you have ever played a game of draw poker. How? Imagine that you are in a game of five-card draw with some college friends. All the players at the table throw in a small ante, say $1 each, in order to start the first hand. The dealer gives you terrible cards, so you fold your hand and give up your ante because your cards give you a signal that your odds of winning are poor. After all, one early hand does not determine if you will be a big winner or a big loser for the evening. In this example, what has really happened? You took a small, defined loss (your $1 ante) in order to insure that you didn't have to take a large, uncontrolled loss that might be a major setback. You made a small mistake, but small mistakes are okay in poker-land. It's large catastrophic disasters that knock you out of the game.

It sounds so simple, but if you are going to win, you must stay in the game. How do you stay in the game? Your keep your chips. How do you keep your chips? You control your losses. If you lose all your chips, you can't even stay in the game, let alone win it. If you lose all your chips, you are done, period. This commandment really hits home after you see a novice investor ride a stock down from $80 to $8, all because he lacked a defensive game plan.

In our poker game example, losing a $1 ante is not great, but it is just a part of the game, and it is far superior to foolishly staying in any single hand of draw poker if you hold bad cards. On any individual hand, if you don't hold the cards that give you the potential to score big, you are better off folding and calling upon your defense to hold your field position and keep you in the game.

Suppose that in our fantasy poker game, you lose your ante six times in a row. Frustration starts to set in, but you stick with your defensive game plan every time you draw a bad hand. If the offense is not in the cards, you play defense. You take care of the downside, with confidence that the upside will eventually show up. Finally, on the seventh hand, the stars are aligned, the cards are aligned, and you draw three kings and two nines, cards that give you the potential for a big winner. You see a fat pitch over the middle of the plate. What do you do? You swing the bat and put some offense back in the game. You call the last bet, you raise it, and you stay in the game in a rational, poker-faced way. You now have upside, an opportunity to win back some money and put some points on the board for the home team. Much like a savvy, seasoned athlete reads a game situation, you now take on more risk (albeit measured risk) because the odds of success are now in your favor.

This is not to imply that stock investing is only a game of chance. Stock investing is a serious enterprise. The point is that success in either stock investing or draw poker depends greatly on risk measurement and risk management. In the first six hands of our poker game analogy, you saw negative signals, you recognized them, and you reacted defensively by folding your cards. On the seventh hand, you drew to a full house, you saw a positive signal, and you reacted to it in a positive way that increased your profit potential. Although the first six pitches were way out of the strike zone, the seventh was right down the middle. When the percentages became favorable, you raised the stakes and played it out. Hopefully, your offense scored some points for your team, but during the early hands, it was definitely your defense and your damage control that kept you in the game.

In today's world, all too often we reward correctness and perfect execution, while we ridicule errors and poor execution. For better or worse, the "perfection mindset" is the reason that many entrepreneurial types are successful. Recognizing this, members of the advertising media constantly promote the perfect car, the perfect getaway, the perfect mate, and ways to get us closer to that elusive perfect life. As sports fans, we have an almost religious regard for the "perfect game," or the "hole-in-one," but we have little time for second place, and virtually no time for losers. If you don't believe that, tell me who finished in second place last year in the "Indy 500," or in the NBA Western Conference "Most Valuable Player" balloting. I don't know, do you?

From several different angles, we are going to attack the thinking that winning is 100% good and losing is 100% bad, because in the real world game of money and markets, there is no justification for that kind of reasoning. Perfection has never been the norm, and it never will be, so get over it. Like some of your favorite athletes, you can be wildly successful by being much less than perfect. Leave your ego and your obsession with perfection in the locker room.

As an investor, learning to live with errors, and with being wrong in the short run, is critical to being right in the long run. No one has perfect forecasting ability, or the ability to avoid losses every time he plays the game. It's not about always avoiding losses, it's about risk management, and surviving when you lose so that you can get closer to each new opportunity to win. It's not about one game, or one possession, or one deal. The important thing is that you work through the bad at-bats, and the poor possessions, and the sad stock selections so that you can stay in the games a long time and become a great success over a long investing career.

In the ring or not, ain't nothing wrong with going down. It's staying down that's wrong.

Muhammad Ali
Former Boxing Champion

Every time we fly across the country in a commercial jet, we exhibit confidence in the total experience we know as air travel. Consciously, or sometimes less than consciously, we hold a high level of confidence in the captain, the crew, the aircraft, the engines, the mechanics, the air flight controllers, and every other detail that goes into the total system known as air travel. We do this because, as rational human beings, we know that air travel is a relatively safe and efficient way to get from point A to point B. We want to get to our destination, arrive safely, and arrive on time. Sure, we could ride a bike on a cross country trip from Los Angeles to New York, but as rational thinkers (who are all too often in a hurry) we usually prefer to go with a system that is quick, tested and efficient versus one that is slow, untested and inefficient. For these reasons, air travel remains a popular choice for traveling over long distances, even though it is less than perfect.

We would agree then, that air travelers have "controlled confidence" in the total system known as flying. If you want to become an all-pro investor, you need to develop a similar level of controlled confidence in a complete system of investing. That confidence can grow into the deep roots of an investing game plan that, over time, can become as important to you as the official game plan of any of today's professional coaches. In fact, your investing game plan may actually become the critical element, and the most important weapon in your investing arsenal. Sticking with the plan will become as important to you as air travel, and it will become much more important to you than some stupid scoreboard that measures wins and losses, or perfection and imperfection.

The year was . . .?

Senior PGA Tour begins play

Nike Corporation goes public

George Brett bats .390 for the full season

Lakers win NBA Championship over Seventy-sixers

Phillies over Royals in World Series

Dow Jones Industrial Average closes the year at 964

The year was . . . 1980.

In the computer world, an operating system like MS Dos™, Windows 98™, or Windows XP™ gives a computer a specific instruction to follow in response to a specific event or set of variables. The operating system is programmed with preconceived and tested responses to various situations, so hesitation is not a part of the programming. Is the personal computer a great thing, or what? If we don't interfere with it, the computer's preprogrammed operating system will lead us to a logical, reasoned response to the situation that it is presented with.

Given the proper training and effort, you can develop a game plan that will work for you like a computer's operating system, one that will give you clarity when the markets seem cloudy and confusing. Think of it as your personal "market operating system," or "M.O.S." While it may not always give you one specific response, it can be pre-programmed with a defined set of risk-control parameters so that it will consistently give you actions to take in response to the specific set of conditions the market throws at you.

The "market operating system" (M.O.S.) is something that most rookie investors have never considered, but trust me on this. If developed properly, a M.O.S. will greatly elevate your level of confidence, and it will put you head and shoulders above the average ego-driven investor. Over time, hesitation and indecision will fade away like a thirty-year-old AA ballplayer. You will experience the truth in the old Wall Street saying that "sometimes you make money by not losing money." Sometimes you "win by not losing." You have all seen the same kind of damage control and operating system surface in sports. A prime example would be a late game situation where Bob Brenly (current Diamondbacks manager) decides not to pitch to Barry Bonds, because it's a one-run ballgame and there's a runner on second base. In a situation like that, the manager is using his book (operating system) on a hitter in an attempt to "win by not losing." A similar combination of discipline, risk measurement, and a "market operating system" can lead to winning by not losing with your stock portfolio.

In the end, there is really only one overriding reason why you should stick with your "market operating system." What's that? If you "don't" stick with your M.O.S., you increase the probability that sooner or later you will fail as an investor. Can anyone, including this writer, measure accurately your increased probability of failure if you do not use a market operating system? Probably not. However, a case can be made that there is a direct, definable correlation between the use of a M.O.S. and the probability of long-term success as an investor. So, if you can just develop and stick with a "market operating system," you can dramatically decrease your chances of failing as an investor. That's the ultimate reward, because if you fail as an investor, you no longer get to suit up for the game. If you lose all your chips, you can't play the game, right? To the player-investor, failure means being busted, broke, and wiped out, which can lead to its own set of additional problems, including serious self-esteem and psychological issues. Who needs that?

When it comes to a "market operating system," you first must face the reality that if you don't know what your operating system is, you probably don't have one. A little sweat equity and time spent reading books like this one is a positive thing that can get you well on your way to defining your own operating system.

* * *

Night after night, his operating system, both mental and physical, is critical to the success or failure of his hockey team. He will never be the fastest skater on the ice, but he comes equipped with a mental operating system that is beyond compare. Sure, he makes more money than 99% of the people on the planet, but he still dials up his internal operating system every time the puck drops. As a veteran, he is more like a well-kept ten-year old Mercedes sedan than a flashy new Jaguar, but that's okay. There is little doubt that most teams in the NHL would sign him in a heartbeat. He is Martin Brodeur, goalie for the New Jersey Devils (and the 2002 Canadian Hockey Team), and a bright star in the constellation known as the National Hockey League.

Great hockey goalies, like Brodeur, have a mental operating system that sports psychologists would love to dissect. NHL goalies can generally "dial it up" mentally to levels that take them off the charts when compared to the rest of us. Sure, they were born with special talents, but their mental energy and intensity helps define them as true professionals. There we go again, talking about another kind of "operating system," because every successful goalie in professional hockey has a "mental operating system" highly superior to most of the rest of us.

Did you ever see a NHL hockey goalie win a game for his team in the first period of play? Hard to say, isn't it? But think about this. An off-balance goalie who fails to "show up" mentally can definitely "lose" a game for his team in the first period of play. As a prime example, look no further than game seven of the 2002 Western Conference Finals, where Patrick Roy of the Avalanche gave up four goals to the Redwings in the first period of play. Was it a fluke? Probably, but things like that can happen to even one of the best if he fails to dial up his mental operating system from the moment the first puck is dropped. Any great goalie brings his mental operating system with him night after night after night, because he knows that if he doesn't, his team can easily be down by two or three goals, and out of the game, before the end of the first period of play. To the great goalie, every game situation means full power, because he knows that the guys on the other side of the puck are among the best in the world at the business of hockey. There is no slow motion on the ice, just as there is no slow motion in the market, so the mental operating system must be engaged and ready to go from the moment the first puck drops.

Let's dig a little deeper into the similarity between large, undisciplined deficits in a hockey game, and large, undisciplined losses in the stock market. Both can lead to insurmountable problems, so in the games of our lives, we would be wise to simply avoid them. Never mask the reality that in sports, as well as in stocks, short-term failure is one possible outcome. That's the way it always has been, and that's the way it always will be. That's why it just makes sense to develop your "market operating system," keep in sharp, and never play a game without it. Mistakes are all right. Disasters are not. Brief mental lapses are bearable. Mental meltdowns are not. Never let one period of play, or one market correction, take you out of the game for good.

* * *

To many fanatics, there is no event in sports as exciting as the home run. Many of the greatest teams in baseball could score runs in bunches, like the Oakland A's of the seventies (Reggie Jackson and company), or the Baltimore Orioles of the eighties (Eddie Murray and company). On the other hand, some of the best teams in baseball history have relied on pitching and defense as key components of their operating system. The Los Angeles Dodgers of the sixties fit this model, with players like Sandy Koufax, Don Drysdale, and Maury Wills. Pitching and defense certainly helped define the Atlanta Braves in the nineties, led by guys like Greg Maddux, Tom Glavine, and Andrew Jones. More recently, the 2001 World Series Champion Arizona Diamondbacks won it all with pitching and defense, courtesy of guys like Randy Johnson, Curt Schilling, and Steve Finley.

Sure, power hitting is electric and helps fill the seats, but the fact remains that most successful big league managers have a high regard for the power of pitching and the discipline of defense. The great coaches often build a balanced team based on a couple of simple truths. First, they know that it is possible for a baseball team to win a game with limited offense, and by getting only one or two or three well-timed hits over the course of the game. Secondly, they also know that, in a game with no clock, it is impossible to dodge your defensive responsibilities. They know that even if the offensive lineup hits five or six home runs, it is impossible to win a complete nine-inning game unless the defense gets the other team out twenty-seven times. You can't win with just a little defense. The offense can heat up or cool down, but the defense of the great teams remains amazingly consistent. (If you ever experienced the frustration of playing on a team that seemed to give up four or five outs every time you were in the field, you know what I mean.)

Amateur investors often get sacked because they go into the game with only a partial plan of attack, and nothing that even closely resembles a complete and efficient market operating system. Like a kid at a carnival, they buy with no specific idea regarding when they will sell if the market happens to hand them a significant profit. In short, they have no exit strategy when it comes to realizing profits. As a result, even if they catch a positive wave that takes one of their stocks up 20% or 30%, they sometimes miss the opportunity to complete the long pass to the open man and put some points on the board. All too often they do nothing to pull the trigger and take profits, which once again, is the wrong thing to do, especially if the stock rolls over.

Hope overtakes reason, because deep down they begin to "hope" that the stock will just go back to its recent highs in order to once again validate the wisdom of their original purchase. Indecision puts a strangle hold on them, and that "indecision" is actually a decision (often a bad one), since it leads to its own set of consequences. If the stock price keeps drifting away from them like a barrel on the ocean, they do nothing because they are frozen by their own indecision. You may have heard it described as "deer in the headlights," or "head buried in the sand," but any way you describe it, it can get ugly. To spectators watching from the stands, it can play out like the game situation where the coach for the home team does nothing to help a struggling young quarterback who is in over his head. If the coach gets stubborn in that kind of situation, it can get nasty for the home team. If a winning stock starts to deteriorate from highly profitable levels, and you freeze, it can get just as ugly for your portfolio.

In any moment of decision, the best thing you can do is the right thing; the next best thing you can do is the wrong thing; and the worst thing is nothing.

Theodore Roosevelt
26th President of the United States

Like a half-dazed boxer in the middle rounds of a heavyweight fight, the stock of a strong company can stall out and hit a choppy period of consolidation. Stocks sometimes get stuck in neutral, like that jabbing, churning period in some fights where neither the challenger nor the title holder can gain enough momentum to take charge. It is not necessarily a period of weakness or strength, but rather a time to just wait it out. Sooner or later the stock will break out of the consolidation with renewed power. The question is, will the renewed momentum be up or down? Will it be a breakout or a breakdown? Don't guess. Wait for the signal the market trend sends you.

Another problem with some RSIs is that they have not taken the time to define the investment weapons that are really important to them. Too often they are lulled into thinking that their most important investment weapon is the high level of information they get from some financial news network, or from a cluster of financial websites. I have to smile every time I see some new ad for "real-time streaming quotes." What good are real time streaming quotes to the online investor, if that investor has limited experience in working with them and interpreting what they mean? The Internet and global satellite communications systems have made information a commodity that is shared by virtually everyone on the planet who takes the time to look for it. Generally accepted market wisdom holds that the stock market "discounts," or takes into consideration, all known financial information. In the Internet era, it is virtually impossible for one investor to compile all known information, let alone appraise it. That's why it may be misguided to think that just one more financial news source or subscriber investment service will give you an investing edge over the rest of the investing public.

Would an attorney be qualified to analyze a seismographic reading of an earthquake? Probably not. Would a pilot be qualified to analyze a geological reading of an underwater oil reserve? Probably not. Would a political consultant be qualified to analyze the cut and quality of a precious gemstone? Probably not. The point here is that "information is not knowledge." Somewhere along the way we all must find the maturity to come to that realization, so it might as well be right now. Studies have shown that investors who subject themselves to a constant diet of financial babble courtesy of the modern media actually perform worse than long-term investors who tune out most of the daily chatter. Do not allow yourself to be swayed into thinking that just a few more hours spent watching cable, or a few more websites, or a couple more investing newsletters, will put you over the top. Information is not knowledge, especially in the age of satellite communications and internet access. Less can be more. Highly filtered, limited, meaningful information can actually give you a high level of comfort and control over your investment decisions.

What is the most important investment weapon you can have, anyway? Is it information? Maybe not, because information only becomes truly valuable when it is combined with the expertise to use it. Any one of us could own a library full of books on a particular subject, but they would be of limited value unless we had the know-how to put that information to practical use in the real world. Information alone is never going to be your most important investing weapon, so don't be lulled into thinking that it is all you need to be an automatic success in the investment markets. The whole world has access to widely similar information. Even if information is as valuable as a supercharged Indy racecar, someone still has to have the expertise to drive it. The way you, as a serious investor, analyze and apply financial news is much more critical than the news itself.

My take is that your most important investing weapon is not information, but rather a high level of inner "self-control" over your emotions as they relate to the information that is available to you. For the successful investor, this weapon includes an ability to simplify and filter critical points of information, an ability to restrain your ego, and an ability to stay the course with a predetermined market operating system. If you can do those things, you can become as valuable to your portfolio as the professional driver of the Indy car that we mentioned above. That's when you become the most important player on the track, and the most important piece of the puzzle.

Like a crafty, competitive pitcher who is past his prime, you should come to the realization that "perfection is overrated." A more meaningful goal for most of us may be to harvest successes from the field of failures in life so that we can just stay in the game. If you play well enough to retain your card as a PGA Tour professional, you retain the right to play in tournaments, and you stay in he game. The big leagues are filled with examples of older, left-handed pitchers who are less than perfect. They just seem to hang around, and by just staying in the game they often experience reasonable success over long careers. In the market, just as in the PGA Tour or in the big leagues, the important thing is to simply stay in the game, because if you can do that, you can also experience reasonable success over a very long career. Who knows, you may experience success like that of a past-his-prime pitcher named Nolan Ryan, who pitched three no-hitters, won 135 games, and struck out 2,465 batters—all after his thirty-fifth birthday.

You see, in the end it is not the "market" that makes you right or wrong. It is not "information" about the market that makes you right or wrong. It is your discipline, your confidence, your focus, and your flexibility that makes you right. These character traits are like loyal assistant coaches who will always be on the sidelines with you. Just as they have helped hundreds who have gone before you, they will help you develop your "market operating system," your game plan, and your rules of engagement. Trust them. Listen to them. Believe in them.

CHAPTER SEVEN:
FIFTY WAS ONCE TEN

In the world of real estate investing, it is often said that the three most important factors to consider when buying a property are "location, location, and location." As strange as it may sound, in the world of stock market investing the three most important elements of success may just be "cut your losses, cut your losses, and cut your losses."

Although risk management and damage control are not the most pleasant topics to study, the mathematical reality is that every 50% loss was at one time a 10% loss. That sounds so elementary, but some rookie investors don't even like to consider the consequences of this possibility. If a stock goes from $100 down to $50, it has to go through $90, right? Thus, any real 50% loss was at one time a 10% loss, and then a 15% loss, and so on. Small, measured losses are not a bad thing, especially if they are taken in response to a specific signal that the market gives you. In hindsight they can look so reasonable. If you play chess, you know that prudent strategy involves sacrificing some of your pawns and rooks in the early tradeoff of the game as a part of the bigger strategy of protecting your bishops and your queen. Much like a chess game, where you make small sacrifices in order to protect your key pieces, you can lose some battles in the market on your way to protecting your key pieces, and ultimately win the match.

An obvious problem in an imperfect world is that if a stock you own drops by 10%, you have no crystal ball to help you forecast its next move. Not one of us has the perfect foresight to always know whether the next move that a stock makes will be up or down. The disciplined investor who cuts his loss at a tight sell level such as minus 10% is taking a stand based on what he knows at that moment. Over the next few days and weeks he might look like a fool, or he might look like a genius. Does that really matter? No, because events like that happen every day in the markets.

What matters is that over long seasons in the market, the odds are that the "disciplined guy," who cuts his losses, will be better off than the "frozen guy," who hides his head in the sand and relies on hope to bring him back to profitability. "Frozen guy" runs the risk of waking up a few months later to the harsh reality that his stock that gave him a sell signal at minus 10% has unraveled by minus 30%, or minus 40%, or minus 50%. Now who looks more foolish? Who feels more foolish? It is not the "disciplined guy" who cut his loss at minus 10%. It's the "frozen guy" who remained on the sidelines, and did nothing while his stock dropped through the floor.

> *When a thing is done, it's done. Don't look back. Look forward to your next objective.*
>
> **George C. Marshall**
> **World War II General, U.S. Army**

Since real players don't lose time worrying about "perfection," let's dig a little deeper into the details of damage control. The section on "offensive strategy" is coming, I promise. Anyway, assuming for a minute that losses were the only possible outcomes, then the first loss (lowest percentage loss) would definitely be the best loss. As we have reviewed, this strategy involves the disciplined use of sell-stop orders at predetermined price levels to protect your capital if a stock starts to break down. As strange as it may sound, to take the first loss, assuming the signal is given by the action in the market, is a proactive strategy that you should come to trust. A defined sell signal will not be perfect every time, but over time it will become your ally. Sure, to some you look like a failure at the moment you take a short-term loss on a stock position that you may have held for only a few days. One short-term loss doesn't matter in the big scheme of things. Taking one loss is like those times when Sammy Sosa takes a swing at a pitch in the dirt. The key is never one pitch, it is to stay in the game in order to get a lot of pitches to hit, because over a complete baseball season a hitter like Sosa will get as many as 2,000 pitches to hit. It's like those times when Bret Farve under-throws a pass for an interception. The secret is not one pass, it is to stay in the game in order to get a lot of opportunities, because over a complete football season a quarterback like Farve will get as many as 700 opportunities to throw a forward pass. Have the mindset of a superior athlete. Hold on to the reality that one negative outcome is never a sign of your ultimate chances for success or failure as an investor.

> *Success is going from failure to failure without losing your enthusiasm.*
>
> **Winston Churchill**
> **Statesman, British Prime Minister**

"Course management" in the game of golf is a great concept because, regardless of talent level, anyone can use it to improve his game. Course management basically involves using your brain to keep you out of trouble, based upon your knowledge of your game and your opponent (the golf course) on any particular day. As a sports discipline, it allows you to neutralize some of your personal playing weaknesses by knowing the terrain of the course you are playing and the best approach for a player with your talent level. If you happen to have an erratic long game, you know that a three wood or a long iron may give you a better chance of keeping it in the short grass on certain holes. This is not advanced calculus, it is more like "catastrophe avoidance." If you have a tendency to slice with your driver, and the next fairway is only thirty yards wide with water on the right, course management dictates that you approach that fairway with a shorter club. By playing the percentage shot, you can actually make the course your ally instead of your adversary. Through a clearer understanding of how the course plays to your strengths and weaknesses, you have a decent chance of getting the most out of the game that you bring to the course on any particular day. If you know golf, the concept of "course management" should help you better identify with all this talk about damage control.

Most of us laugh at baseball bloopers, but in reality we would do almost anything to avoid being placed in those types of situations. We have been conditioned from our days in youth sports to think of a loss, or a blooper, or an error as a signal of weakness. Remember the routine grounder that went through Bill Buckner's legs in the tenth inning of the sixth game of the 1986 World Series? If you've seen it once, you've seen it twenty times. Buckner was a fine player over a long career with the Boston Red Sox who happened to make an error at a critical time in a critical game. It was only one play in the baseball game of life, and it should be remembered that way. Sadly, it probably never will be.

We can learn a lot from the kid's game of tug-of-war. The market price of a stock at any one moment is the result of a complex battle that in some ways resembles a tug-of-war between the economic forces we know as supply and demand. Every two-sided transaction in an auction marketplace must have a buyer and a seller. Each buyer represents the "demand team," and each seller represents the "supply team." The battle plays out like a tug-of-war, with thousands of participants on each end of the rope who are all attempting to pull (buy or sell) in the direction that will benefit their team. In the supply-demand tug-of-war known as the stock market, the other players in the game basically have no regard for your feelings. They never will. Don't take it personally, because that's just the way it is. Develop enough discipline to take a "first loss" in the neighborhood of nine to 10%. Remain aware that a greater loss is always a possibility, not because of something you did, but as a result of conditions and events that are out of your control and out of your vision. In a fluid marketplace, specific stock prices move every day as a result of events that very few players were able to predict in advance. Practice course management. Sometimes you have to cut your losses and move on to the next tee box. If you can accept strategies that involve taking a "first loss" at a predetermined exit point, then you won't compound one bad decision (the purchase of a stock prior to a decline) by making a second bad decision (holding and hoping).

Imagine you are Mike Shanahan, the head coach of the Denver Broncos, in the final game of the regular season. Here's the situation. If you win, you go the first round of the playoffs with accolades for you and the team. If you lose, you go fishing. You have possession of the ball, you are down by two points, and there is only one minute left in the game. The good news is that you have the ball, third and goal, on the other team's six-yard line. Talk about great field position. This is not the time for wild, heroic behavior. After all, you have a strong chance to take your team to the playoffs. All you have to do is score a field goal and you win. Three points would be great, but seven points would really not be any better, because either way you accomplish your goal of winning the game. This is a situation where the correct call on third-and-goal is a conservative, high probability play. It is no time for a drop-back pass play, because if your guys take too much time to get the play off, they risk a quarterback sack or an interception. The right decision is to stay conservative, call a high percentage play on third down, and let your players execute. This is no time for you, as the head coach, to get fancy. Your mission will be accomplished if you run the ball, establish ball placement near the center of the field, and let your kicker win the game with a field goal on fourth down. If it plays out that way, you win the game by one point and you go to the playoffs.

There is nothing complex about the decision-making process that we have just outlined. It could simply be called, "high probability actions when there is a lot on the line." That simple statement may be one of the seven wonders of the investment world. Alan Shaw, head of the technical research department at a major investment firm, has an amazingly direct approach to this subject of "potential risk and potential reward." He breaks down and defines the only four things that can happen to a stock investment as follows:

it can go up a little,
it can go up a lot,
it can go down a little, or
it can go down a lot.

Simple, but straight. If a stock goes up a little, that is a good thing for the bullish investor. No problem. If it goes up a lot, there is a plan for that contingency, which includes scaling out of partial positions at various profit levels (more in Section Three: The Offense). If a stock goes down a little, and your signals continue to tell you to hold it as a quality investment, you can live with that. But that fourth event, when a stock goes down a lot, is the one of the four that you, as a successful investor, must avoid. If you don't avoid the "down-a-lots," you may end up feeling the anguish and the anger of a head coach who calls a high-risk play at a critical time in a critical game. You may fail so badly that the scars stay with you deep into the next season. Don't do it. Don't call a high-risk play that can result in a devastatingly negative outcome. Do not hold a stock that deteriorates past the "down-a-little" stage. Use sell-stop orders religiously for every position you own. If you don't, you may get by all right for a while in a bull market. In fact, you may get by for three or four years, like the day traders in the glory days of the late nineties. But, sooner or later, you will suffer from a "down-a-lot" stock, and it will flatten you like a hit from Ray Lewis.

Sure, you may survive the hit to your account balance, but the memory of that "down-a-lot" stock will linger, like the memory of a poor play that should never have been called in the first place. Trust me on the fact that those "down-a-lot" losses can haunt you for a long time. Never let one play, or one position, bury you. Small mistakes are okay. Large disasters are not. Make it one of your primary goals to go through entire seasons with no "down-a-lot" losses, and you will be on the right track.

The year was . . .?

Notre Dame is #1 in the final NCAA college football poll
Raiders over Vikings in Super Bowl
The Apple II, the first successful personal computer, is introduced
Reggie Jackson hits three home runs in game 6 of the World Series
Oakland over Minnesota in Super Bowl
The motion picture Star Wars debuts
Dow Jones Industrial Average closes the year at 831

The year was . . . 1977.

With that in mind, it is often best to keep any past prejudices regarding the reputation of any specific corporation out of the equation. Remain objective, and don't be swayed by the past or present strength of the specific company. Focus on the present strength of the "stock" as it relates to all the other stocks that are available to you in the marketplace. View any stock that you are considering for purchase like you would view a young, untested draft choice with a lot of untested potential. Note that I said untested potential. Don't get fooled by the name recognition, or the past track record of a company, without completely checking out its current fundamental and technical credentials (as described in detail in Section Three). Never buy a stock just because you like its products, or its promotional clips. History supports the fact that highly admired companies with stellar performance records can become very poor stock investments over certain windows of time.

Consider this. He batted .181 and hit six home runs in 1935 for the Boston Braves. The player was . . .?

How about this one? He hit .211 and hit six home runs in 1973 for the New York Mets. The player was . . .?

Any fan locked in a time warp would not think very highly of these stats, or these players. The stats are obviously sub-par, but the names of the players might surprise you. The fact is that the numbers above help record the final years in the careers of Babe Ruth (1935, Boston Braves), and Willie Mays (1973, New York Mets), respectively.

Like an old all-star whose reputation is stronger than his skills, there is sometimes a "disconnect" between the reputation of a great company and the way its stock is trading in the open marketplace. You must constantly be on guard for this phenomenon, and avoid hanging onto old emotions about a company just because you like what it makes, or what it does. Do not own a stock just because your grandfather owned it, or because you have some positive memory about the underlying corporation. Ruth and Mays were fine players over long careers, but they did little to help their respective teams in those 1935 and 1973 seasons.

Besides, the so-called favorite doesn't always win the contest. In sports, that's why we play it out, rather than just declaring a winner after analyzing the two opposing teams "on paper." One of the great wonders about sports is the opportunity to play the game. We don't just study it, we experience it. The Las Vegas odds-makers had Muhammed Ali as a seven to one underdog prior to his first heavyweight title fight against Sonny Liston (Ali won the fight). The 1968 New York Mets finished ninth in the National League, and won only seventy-three games. As a result, the 1969 team was a huge underdog at the start of the next season, the year when the "miracle Mets" went on to beat perennial favorite Baltimore in the World Series. So much for the accuracy of projections "on paper."

Infamous stock market examples prove the point that the prior reputation of a great company is of little value when determining whether or not it will turn out to be a great stock to own. XYZ Corporation can be a great company at exactly the same time that it is a not-so-great stock investment. Over specific windows of time, the stock of a highly reputable company can disconnect from that company, and become a very poor equity investment.

For years, AT&T was considered to be one of the bluest of the blue chips, and even a great stock for widows and orphans. Somewhere along the way that all changed. At the end of 1991, the stock was trading around $13. During the 1990s, it went up over 300%, to a price above $60, only to fall all the way back to the $13 area by the end of the decade. Post script: as of mid-year 2002, it is now trading around $10. You might want to keep this in mind as an example of why you should do your own research before you get attached to your grandfather's stocks.

Consider the case of IBM in the mid-1990s. It was a leading technology company, included in the Dow Jones Industrial Average, and in terms of total capitalization it was one of the ten largest companies in the United States. The years 1996 and 1997 were reasonably positive ones for the U.S. stock market. In 1996 and 1997 combined the S&P 500 Index rose over 50% (1996 22.9%, 1997 33.3%). Nevertheless, from early 1996 through the end of 1997, IBM common stock was a sub-par performer, to say the least. During that period the stock dropped 22% in value, from a price of $41 in 1996 to $32 by late 1997. Again, this minus 22% performance occurred during a period when the market rose more than 50%. Suppose you were the "blind-faith" guy who bought 2000 shares of IBM in 1997 at $41 per share, and then put it in a file and did nothing to monitor it. On paper, in less than twenty-four months you lost $18,000 ($82,000 investment minus $64,000 ending value equals $18,000 loss), or 22% of your original investment, and this all occurred during a bull market. Over that specific time frame, there is no arguing the fact that you owned a strong, highly reputable company, but the record shows that you owned a very weak, highly unprofitable stock investment.

Some self-proclaimed market experts even go so far as to recommend that certain established, reputable, blue chip companies should be defined as "one-decision stocks." The description is self-explanatory. In theory, at least, since these stocks should be able to weather any and all future economic conditions, the only decision that needs to be made is the single decision regarding when to buy them. In the opinion of these market wizards, since these stocks should never be sold, a "sell decision" will never need to be made.

This "blind faith" investing approach is simply not sound business practice, and in the modern marketplace you don't have to look very far to find the fallacy in the concept of "one-decision stocks." Periods of broad underperformance have affected numerous "one-decision stocks" over the past five years. Consider the following examples. Procter and Gamble, from its high price in 2000 of $118 to its low price the next year of $56, dropped 52%. From a high of $70 in 2000, Wal-Mart fell 40% to a low of $42 the next year. Finally, AT&T fell from grace, and in value, from a 1999 high of more than $60, to a 2002 low of around $10. That, my friends, was a 77% decline.

Be forewarned. Since even great companies can hit huge air pockets, it is advisable for you to constantly scout the talent of each of the stocks that make up your portfolio. In the global economy of this new century, there is no such thing as a one-decision stock. As noted earlier, it is best to determine an "uncle" point for every equity position you buy. Cut your losses at around 9% and step aside if that becomes necessary. Never hold and hope, because if the forces of the market start to come down on you, you may not be able to neutralize them. Just as a sound defensive team "contains" a star running back, you can "contain" the opponent we call the market. Containing in either case means giving up small, defined losses, in order to avoid giving up large devastating losses. If you are focused and flexible enough to contain whatever the opponent brings at you, you will be just fine.

During times of chaos, even the most basic military strategy stresses action over inaction. When military recruits receive training regarding what to do during extreme combat situations, they are taught to either advance or retreat, but not to freeze in their tracks. If they can advance, fine. If they must retreat, they are trained to cut their losses in order to be able to fight another day. A wounded soldier who retreats is of far greater value than a stubborn one who charges ahead and doesn't survive the experience. When put in the proper perspective, a retreat can be a positive course of action for even the most courageous.

I made up my mind, but I made it up both ways.

Casey Stengel
Former Yankees Manager

Although it's humorous at first glance, this is not the kind of advice that will get you very far when you invest in the market. Sure, the temptation to sit on the fence strikes all of us from time to time. Don't do it. Don't make up your mind both ways, or right down the middle. When it comes to protecting your investment principal, follow the lead of a great defensive linebacker like Ray Lewis, or a great defensive shortstop like Omar Vizquel, or a great defensive catcher like Ivan (Pudge) Rodriguez. Work hard to develop your offense, but take pride in your defense and never let your guard down. Strive to be one of the "golden glove" investors in your league, and do not hesitate to take the "first loss" if the signals are there.

Timeout. No more negative talk for a minute. I admit that we seem to be spending an inordinate amount of time discussing ways to protect your backside. We do this, not because of a pessimistic bias, but because of the positive, upside potential provided by one of the greatest financial wonders of the free world, the U.S. stock market. Never forget that it is possible to generate very real, life-changing profits by investing in stocks over extended periods of time. The U.S. stock market has a positive upward bias. If this were not the case, the averages would be at zero, right? As further proof, consider that the Dow Jones Industrial Average, the most popular measure of the value of blue-chip stocks, traded at a level of 42 in 1931. In 2002 it traded above 10,000. That increase in value, when combined with reinvested dividends, equates to an average annual return in excess of 10.5%. Public ownership in common stock is higher than it has ever been in our history, which is as it should be. Sure, there have been speed bumps along the way, but the all-American systems we know as capitalism and free enterprise have produced real quality of life changes for countless American investors. I have witnessed it first-hand, by knowing clients who own Microsoft with a cost basis of less than $6 a share (approximate value of Microsoft common as of June 2002 was $45 per share), or Home Depot with a cost basis of less than $9 a share (approximate value of Home Depot common as of June 2002 was $40 per share).

Yes, we focus on defense here, not to be overly negative, but to protect the positives provided by this great asset class. As a country, we often focus on defense, not to be overly negative, but to protect the positives provided by our great way of life. I hope we can all live with that.

CHAPTER EIGHT:

THE NIGHTMARE KNOWN AS NEGATIVE COMPOUNDING

You probably have heard of the "rule of 72," a simple rule of thumb regarding positive compounding. If you divide the annual rate of return into the fixed number seventy-two, the result is the approximate number of years required to "double your investment." For instance, if you earn an annual return on your money of 9%, it will take you approximately eight years to double your money (seventy-two divided by nine equals eight years).

Be ever aware of the fact that just as money compounds on the way up, it also compounds on the way down. If a stock's momentum turns negative, and you do nothing to protect your principal, the value of your portfolio can break down like a castle in the sand.

The year was . . .?

Forty-niners defeat Bengals in the Super Bowl
The Exxon Valdez incident is the worst oil spill in U.S. history
Pistons over Lakers for NBA Championship
Pete Rose is banned from baseball for life
Calgary defeats Montreal for the Stanley Cup
Dow Jones Industrial Average closes the year at 2,753

The year was . . . 1989.

Every team is in first place on opening day. What a great feeling. It's the feeling you have on the day that you buy a stock. Justifiably, you hope for future pleasure, and you haven't felt any pain. You feel the way Cubs fans feel on opening day, year after year after year. The following numbers might be compared to the reality of early season losing streaks, and the struggle that is required to claw your way back up the ladder towards first place.

If you invest $10,000 in a new stock position, and you are forced to sell it at a loss of 7.5%, then you need to make back only 8.1% to get back to break even. We could compare that to losing a couple of games early, and then making them up during the next weekend series.

If you lose 9% from your inception price, then you must make back only 9.9% to get back up to your original level of investment.

If you lose 10% on the same $10,000 stock position, then you must make 11.1% to get back to even. Most of us can live with that possibility, and at this level we would still be high in the standings.

Now let's consider some bigger draw-downs. If you allow a $10,000 stock position to deflate by 20%, you must then make 25% to get back to even. At this point you're in an investment air pocket where the discomfort starts to get serious for most rookie investors.

If you lose 30%, then you must make back 43% just to get back to the level of your original investment. These numbers start to reflect the magnitude of negative compounding. You might compare this type of loss to the unsettling frustration of a blowout football game where your team is down by twenty-eight points in the third quarter. Although it's not impossible to come back from a deficit this large, it's certainly not easy.

If you lose 40%, then you must make 66% to make it back to your original investment.

If you lose 50%, then you need to make an even 100% to get back to your original investment. A loss this large severely limits your ability to recover, to say the least.

Loss of Principal	**Required Return**
-7.5%	**+8.1%**
-9%	**+9.9%**
-10%	**+11.1%**
-20%	**+25.0%**
-30%	**+43.0%**
-40%	**+66.0%**
-50%	**+100.0%**

Percentage return required to completely recover specific losses of principal.

* * *

A problem created by numbers this large is that, whether you're dealing with football plays or stock plays, players and coaches who get down by a huge deficit often feel the urge to take greater than average risk in an effort to get back in the game. We have all seen it play out in sports. One team, down by twenty-eight late in the third quarter, starts to force things and ends up falling further behind because of high-risk pass plays and poor execution. In the case of fallen investors or money managers, they often end up taking greater incremental risks in an effort to play catch up, and improve their performance relative to the popular averages. Although this higher-risk strategy sometimes works, many times it backfires.

The investment ocean has pulled a countless number of investors under water, never to be heard from again. Rather than "extreme sports," these guys experience the pain of something we might just as well call "extreme negative compounding."

You might even want to post these two rules in your workout area. Rule number one: don't set yourself up so that one stock position or one unforeseen market event can flatten you. ("Don't let one punch take you out.")

Rule Number Two: never forget rule number one.

Anyone knows that fifteen plus fifteen is thirty, right? If you are pulling back up after a big investment loss, there is a time when the numbers don't work out. Specifically, after a net loss of 30%, two consecutive gains of 15% will **not** get you back to even. Go ahead and call it a trick question, but let's take a look at the numbers. If you start with a round number like $100,000 and draw it down by 30%, you then have only $70,000 of remaining equity. From that level, if you gain 15%, you are back up to $80,500. If you gain 15% again from that new level, you have only increased your equity back up to $92,575. The reality is that after a loss of 30%, you are in such a hole that even two very acceptable gains of 15% will not get you back to the account value that you started with ($92,575 versus $100,000).

Like a raging bull (or bear), uncontrolled negative volatility can wreck an unprotected stock portfolio. Consider just one final perspective on this thorny issue of volatility. If you start with a portfolio valued at $100,000, make a positive return of 80% in year one, then lose a negative 50% in year two, are you up or down from your original $100,000?

You were plus eighty, then minus fifty. The net result has got to be positive, right? Wrong. The result is that your total return on this portfolio would still be negative. Based on a $100,000 starting value, an account that somehow grew at an 80% annual rate would have a value of $180,000 after year one. The problem surfaces in this hypothetical example because, at a rate of minus 50% in year two, that $180,000 value would be sliced to $90,000. After two years of Rolaids™ and rolling all around the spreadsheet, you would still have less money than you started with.

Wild performance swings like the ones mentioned above may remind you of some big league pitching staffs. Imagine the frustration of managing a major league ball club with a starting rotation made up of one legitimate ace, one above average pitcher, and two guys who are so erratic that they should be in AA ball. That inconsistent mix of talent would make it almost impossible to know what to expect from day to day. "Highly volatile" usually leads to highly uncomfortable. When given the choice, most managers would probably opt for a more stable rotation made up of four above-average starters with consistently good stuff. That mix of starters would at least give the team "order" instead of "chaos," and a legitimate chance of winning every time the team stepped on the field. You will do well to consider methods that mirror those of the consistent, above-average pitching rotation.

In recent years, "Survivor" has become a huge hit for the CBS television network. The reality of the game is played out in the form of challenges where action is often much more important than analysis. Survivor want-to-be's usually have little time to make decisions. Like the members of the wild kingdom that they sometimes share space-with, the best players often seem to have a reflexive ability to see a situation, read it, and react to it. Decisiveness, as much as quickness, often plays a huge role in the "Survivor" mentality of the best players.

He who walks in the middle of the road, gets hit from both sides.

George P. Schultz

Former U.S. Secretary of State

In many ways, the best "survivors" on Wall Street share the decisive, heroic traits of the best survivors on the reality TV show. They realize that the market has no regard for their feelings, and they kill losing trades early before the trades have a chance to hurt them. If an investment is a bad idea, they recognize that fact, they kill it, and they bury it. After all, a bad idea is a bad idea. Admit it. Kill it. Dust yourself off. Move on. For serious investors like us, moving out of a situation that gives a negative signal is heroic because that kind of decisive action gives us more ammunition (money) for the next battle. And that ammunition, like food and water, is critical to our ultimate investment survival.

Make me wise in the ways of the old antelope. What do I mean by that? In the wilds of Africa, an antelope has many enemies, namely carnivorous ones like lions, leopards, and tigers. Sure, all antelopes have reasonable speed and agility, but in a "survival of the fittest" world, the strongest and fastest and keenest survive the longest. They are the ones that react to danger without hesitation. For that reason, when comparing experience in the marketplace to experience in the jungle, I will take the ways of the wise, old antelope that has lived a long life. If he is old, then he must have a keen ability to recognize danger and react to it. The old antelope is, by definition, a survivor. He has lived through the best and the worst, with wisdom, focus, and flexibility. Let him be a model for all of us who aspire to be "survivor-investors."

If you're into aviation, you know the importance of a pilot's checklist, a tool that helps the pilot keep vital information at his fingertips. A professional pilot completes his preflight checklist, not some of the time, but all the time. The disciplined use of a checklist is critical to the process, like the playbook that we have described so many times. Taking a lead from aviation, we will present an investing checklist for the "offense," the "defense," and the "special teams," each of the three segments of investing that are critical to the successful completion of your personal investing journey.

Use each of these three checklists like the guy in the cockpit. Copy them, make notes on them, and take them with you on each leg of your trip.

Checklist: The Defense

1. In the modern markets, active management has advantages over passive management. If the signal is there, take action.
2. Insure every stock you own against catastrophic loss. Use protective sell-stop orders on every position in the range of minus 9% to minus 10%.
3. Kill your losers; feed your winners.
4. Investing is not about "perfect." Perfect does not exist in the world of the successful investor.
5. Every 50% loss was at one time a 10% loss. Avoid the down-a-lot's.
6. Develop your own "Market Operating System" and follow it. Your action (response) is always more important than the action of the market.
7. There is no such thing as a one-decision stock in the modern global marketplace. The past reputation of a "company" is of little value in determining the future value of a "stock."
8. Offense wins games, but defense wins championships.

Now we move on to the offense. Before we do, take one more moment to reflect on the greatness of the defense. Then move on, enjoying every minute of the game as we prepare to get the ball back.

SECTION THREE: THE OFFENSE (A MEETING WITH THE OFFENSIVE COORDINATOR)

CHAPTER NINE:
THE OFFENSIVE FOUNDATION

Better to do a little well than a great deal badly.

Socrates,
Greek Philosopher

Do a few things well. Spend your time and your energy on those things. Hang around those things. That's one take on the ancient wisdom of Socrates. That simple approach may be a very valid logical way to go about the job of building an offensive team of stocks to make up your portfolio, so if simple works, stay with it. Complex is overrated, anyway, because complexity can become a burden that ultimately undermines your chances for financial success in the stock market. Do a few things well, and hang around those things. The idea could just as easily come from an ancient Greek philosopher, or a modern day athletic coach.

One simple, but effective, way to develop a great stock portfolio is to compare the job to the development of a great sports franchise. For starters, look no farther than the structure of your favorite pro football team. Since I can't read your mind, let's take a look at a perennially strong football franchise from San Francisco. Loved by some and hated by others, the Forty-niners franchise has enjoyed a tremendously high level of success over the past twenty years, winning 68% of their regular season games over that period (1982-2001, regular season record 216 wins, ninety-six losses). We all have watched them win numerous playoff games on the way to winning four Super Bowl titles over the past two decades. That is most definitely a tribute to the organization, and a salute to its greatness. The franchise is currently owned by the DeBartolo Corporation, and in the classic flow of an organizational chart, the day-to-day management of the Forty-niners is the responsibility of Terry Donahue, the team's general manager. Donahue is the key piece of the management pyramid, and he has surrounded himself with head coach Dennis Erickson, as well as other fine coaches and scouts.

The Debartolo Corporation has empowered Donahue and his staff with player selection and development responsibilities. These are variables that are critical to the financial success and field success of the San Francisco Forty-niners franchise, so every off-season, consideration must be given to the careers of current roster players like Jeff Garcia, Terrell Owens, and Dana Stubblefield, as well as hundreds of free agents and draft-eligible college players, in an effort to create a success equation for the upcoming season.

This player selection process involves comparative screening techniques, composite ratings systems, and digging deep in an effort to separate real value from hype and perceived value. This selection process is critical, not just one time, but season after off-season after season. Players change, talent levels change, teams change, but the desire to win never changes in the National Football League. So Terry Donohue, like every other general manager in the NFL, seeks to balance player forecasts with profit projections. He constantly strives to find a point of equilibrium between projections regarding future value and the cost of securing those assets (players). Due to the salary cap and other financial constraints, he does not have the luxury of spending money foolishly. His is a serious business.

The year was . . .?

Georgetown defeats Houston for NCAA basketball championship
Dell Computer is founded by college dropout, Michael Dell
L.A. Raiders defeat Redskins in the Super Bowl
Celtics over Lakers for NBA title
Dow Jones Industrial Average closes the year at 1,212

The year was . . . 1984.

In the mind of the general manager, what are the key elements of the success equation? They include balancing needs with resources, as well as routine player selection, player development, and player monitoring. Each season, the Forty-niners' brain trust, like that of every other team in the NFL, seeks a reasonable balance of veteran talent, free-agent talent, and rookie talent, in an effort to create a blend that has a high probability for success.

The process includes the creation of balanced subsets of key players that have special abilities in the areas that we know as offense, defense, and special teams, with each having a unique and justifiable role. No team would realistically go into a season with fifteen strong offensive linemen, fifteen strong wide receivers, and no proven quarterback. That makes no sense, and would leave the team with a blind spot.

Balance, straight out of the first chapter of the book of life, is the constant, and the critical ingredient that gives the veteran general manager an advantage over less experienced opponents, because he has years of experience creating rosters that exhibit strength at every link. In an effort to insulate his team from the risk of loss and embarrassment, he must search out high quality pieces for every gap in the player position puzzle.

As much as he may like a high-powered passing offense, one of the worst things a general manager could do is draft too many skill position players without drafting enough talent to protect them. The offensive line protects the skill players. The skill players put points on the board for the benefit of the offensive linesmen (as well as everyone else on the team). A mix of players with no balance is like a mini-portfolio made up completely of technology stocks. The goal of the team concept is to seek broad diversification to fill a broad spectrum of needs. Only after the selection of offensive, defensive, and special teams players does any collection of players start to resemble a complete, balanced team.

The development and makeup of your private stock portfolio should be modeled after the diversification found on a successful sports team like the Forty-niners. As a result of the discipline known as "modern portfolio theory," it is generally accepted that a diversified stock portfolio should include a minimum of eight to ten distinctly different companies that represent different sectors of our economy. A collection of at least ten different companies immediately adds balance to the equity asset class. While a portfolio that includes ten different companies will never be completely insulated from market risk, at that level it would be concentrated, but at least somewhat diversified.

Since we agree that diversification by economic sector is the foundation of a balanced stock portfolio, let's start the selection process by noting thst the benchmark S&P 500 Equity Index represents ten completely distinct economic sectors, almost like separate cylinders that power our economy. By name, these sectors include consumer discretionary, consumer staples, energy, financials, health care, industrials, information technology, materials, telecommunications services, and utilities.

As indicated below, these ten sectors include some great American companies.

Economic Sector	Representative Companies
1. consumer discretionary	General Motors, Ford
2. consumer staples	Coca-Cola, Gillette
3. energy	Exxon Mobil, Chevron Texaco
4. financials	Bank of America, Fannie Mae
5. health care	Merck, Pfizer
6. industrials	General Electric, Boeing
7. information technology	Microsoft, IBM
8. materials	Alcoa, International Paper
9. telecomm services	Cisco Systems, SBC Comm.
10. utilities	Con Ed, Southern Company

With a little creative license, a valid comparison can be made between the major sectors of the U.S. economy and the major positions of play on a football team. In a strikingly similar structure, a matrix of key football team subsets, and specific positions within those subsets might look like this:

Position Sector:	Specific Positions:
1. defensive linesmen	defensive tackle, defensive end, nose-guard
2. linebackers	middle linebacker, outside linebacker
3. defensive backs	cornerback, strong safety, free safety
4. skill backs	quarterback, running back, fullback
5. offensive linesmen	center, guard, tackle
6. receivers	tight end, wide receiver
7. kickers	punter, place kicker
8. special teams	kick return man, defensive hitman

This comparison of from eight or ten positions on a balanced team, and around ten sectors in a balanced economy, has some interesting similarities. It is a way for you, the sports fan, to better identify with the concept of a structured, diversified portfolio. The following chart builds further on the similarity between the team concept and the economic sector concept:

Position Sector	Economic Sector	Representative Companies
1.defensive linesmen	consumer	General Motors
2. linebackers	energy	Exxon Mobil
3. defensive backs	financials	Bank of America
4. offensive backs	healthcare	Merck
5. offensive linesmen	industrials	General Electric
6. receivers	information tech.	Microsoft
7. kickers	materials	Alcoa
8. special teams	telecomm services	SBC Communications

The benefit to a blended portfolio chosen from a matrix like this is that the various companies represent a broad range of business types.

Much like the eleven players on the football field at any given time represent different skill-sets, companies from different sectors of our economy represent different pockets of strength, which adds a positive level of diversification and balance to any portfolio. Health care companies often react to various real world market events in ways that are different from other sectors, such as financial services companies. Technology companies often react to various market events in ways that differ from other sectors, such as transportation companies. In many ways every member of the team helps watch the backside of the other members of the team.

A big league shortstop has a skill-set that differs from that of a big league catcher, yet each player's unique skills increase the chances that the team will ultimately be successful. It happens all the time in baseball. We sometimes see a center fielder, like Bernie Williams, on a hitting tear while a first baseman, like Jason Giambi, is in a hitting slump. That's life. That's sports. That's the essence of the team concept. Time and time again, when one player is struggling, certain other players "pick him up" by sharpening their level of play during that particular stretch of the season. The various companies in a diversified portfolio can do the same thing to pick up the performance of the master portfolio.

As you draft and design a playoff-caliber stock portfolio, consider the blueprint used by your favorite sports franchise, one that emphasizes players with diversified skill sets, and you will be off to a strong start.

Put all good eggs in one basket, and then watch that basket.

Andrew Carnegie
Capitalist, early 1900s

When it comes to portfolio development, reasonable diversification is a cornerstone concept, while sometimes a good thing can be taken too far. Extreme over-diversification, which for purposes of our discussion is defined as carrying fifty or more stocks in a portfolio, may prove to be difficult to monitor, and may not even add that much to the incremental stability of a portfolio. In fact, over-diversification may actually prove to be a drag on performance during certain phases of the market. Extreme over-diversification, that is, the act of holding fifty, or sixty, or seventy stocks in a portfolio, can lead to diminishing returns, that point where each additional position does little or nothing to add to the actual diversification of the portfolio.

The enrollment in the flagship public high school in my hometown is extremely large, to say the least (Texas Class 5-A, the largest classification in Texas). When the varsity football team takes the field for a home game, fans usually witness a herd of eighty to ninety players running out of the tunnel. While it is highly commendable for the coaching staff to allow ninety players to suit up for home games, this mega-number doesn't do much to add to the total field strength of the team, since only eleven players can be in the game at one time. Granted, the head coach probably has a great feel for the talent level of his top twenty to twenty-five players, but can he truthfully make any major distinction between the 83rd guy on the roster and the 84th guy on the roster?

The issue of mega-diversification becomes apparent when you review the quarterly reports of some of the largest growth mutual funds in the country. As of March 31, 2002, the Fidelity Magellan Fund owned stock in 239 different companies. As of that same date, American Funds Growth Fund of America owned stock in 198 different companies. Let me say that these are both very highly regarded mutual funds. However, even with that in mind, how excited would you be to buy the stock ranked 83rd on any mutual fund's buy list? Doesn't that question sound strangely similar to our earlier questions about that high school football team that carries ninety players on the roster? If you would not put your 83rd player into a football game in a critical, game-on-the-line situation, why would you place great faith in the stock ranked 83rd on a mutual fund's buy list?

A more prudent approach to portfolio management is to design a diverse but concentrated portfolio made up of twenty to thirty great American companies that just happen to do business all around the world. Remember, we don't really invest in one stock market or one stock exchange, we invest as part owners in a limited group that includes some of the great business franchises of the world.

The art of being wise is the art of knowing what to overlook.

William James
Psychologist, Author

Where should you start? Just like the NFL general manager who constantly searches for talent and value, you need a defined rating system to help you identify a universe of high quality, established companies that may qualify for your stock portfolio. The first potential problem is that there are currently more than eight thousand public companies that trade on the various domestic stock exchanges. This is anything but a manageable number; just the thought of 8,000 publicly traded stocks represents a prime example of the "information overload" problem that we all face each and every day.

How can you filter this number down to a more manageable universe of companies? Recognizing that size can be one indicator of financial quality, and that quality often prevails over time, one logical starting point is to filter the total number of public companies by capitalization, that is, the total market value of each company. This way you emphasize companies that are large, battle-tested, and in at least some measurable ways, financially stable. Since they are mature businesses, they have good bloodlines, and a history of surviving various economic peaks and valleys.

To implement this stock filtering process, a logical first step is to focus on the 100 largest companies based in the United States. These companies represent some of the all-pro players within the marketplace, and are highly scrutinized by the various organizations that provide stock research to the public. While all of them are not household names, most of them are recognizable because of the important role they play in our overall economy. In today's marketplace, a draft list of the 100 largest publicly traded U.S. companies would include companies with a market capitalization greater than $22 billion. This list, while obviously subject to change, would currently range in size from General Electric (approximate total capitalization of $300 billion) to International Paper (approximate total capitalization of $22.5 billion).

Let's further examine the broad sweep of the companies that we have included in this large-cap draft list. Since the S&P 500 Equity Index is weighted by capitalization (company size), the top names on the list represent major drivers of the U.S. economy. It is somewhat similar to our popular election system, and the resultant power that certain states have over our electoral system. The most populous states like New York, California, Texas, and Florida have the most electoral votes, and thus the most clout in determining our President. Small population states like North Dakota, Nebraska, and Wyoming play a role, but a lesser role. Similarly, because of the capitalization weighting of the S&P 500, large companies like General Electric, Microsoft, and Wal-Mart have a much greater impact on the movement of the Index than smaller companies like Reebok, Centex, and Black and Decker.

Consider this reality, based on current market levels of just the 100 largest U.S. companies:

The companies in the S&P 500 Index make up approximately 80% of the total dollar value of all of the publicly traded companies of the U.S.

The largest 100 companies in the S&P 500 Index represent approximately 80% of the total capitalization of all the 500 companies that comprise the Index.

The net result is that the largest 100 companies in the S&P 500 Index represent approximately 64% of the total capitalization of all the U.S. companies that trade publicly.

Working knowledge of these facts is huge. It is one key to a better understanding of how you can monitor a very significant part of the total U.S. economy through the tracking of a very "manageable" universe of 100 or so specific companies. Focused analysis and study of a relatively small number of corporations will allow you to be in touch with trends that affect a huge percentage of the business that drives our economy. Strictly by the numbers, a subset of 100 companies, out of a total of the eight thousand publicly traded U.S. companies, represents less than two percent of the names, yet those 100 names represent around 64% of the total dollar value of the U.S. market. Now we're on our way to filtering a very unmanageable number down to a very manageable number.

As of this writing (June 2002), the largest 100 U.S. companies in the S&P 500 Equity Index, in rank order, are the following:

1.	General Electric	GE
2.	Microsoft	MSFT
3.	Exxon Mobil	XOM
4.	Pfizer	PFE
5.	Wal-Mart	WMT
6.	Citigroup	C
7.	Intel	INTC
8.	American International Group	AIG
9.	International Business Machine	IBM
10.	Johnson and Johnson	JNJ
11.	Cisco Systems	CSCO
12.	Merck	MRK
13.	Verizon Communications	VZ
14.	SBC Communications	SBC
15.	Home Depot	HD
16.	Coca-Cola	KO
17.	AOL Time Warner	AOL
18.	Philip Morris	MO
19.	Procter and Gamble	PG
20.	Berkshire Hathaway	BRKA

21.	Bank of America	BAC
22.	Chevron Texaco	CVX
23.	Oracle	ORCL
24.	Abbott Laboratories	ABT
25.	PepsiCo	PEP
26.	Bristol-Myers Squibb	BMY
27.	Wyeth Laboratories	WYE
28.	Lilly and Company	LLY
29.	Fannie Mae	FNM
30.	Wells Fargo	WFC
31.	Bellsouth	BLS
32.	Dell Computer	DELL
33.	J.P. Morgan Chase	JPM
34.	Viacom	VIA
35.	United Parcel Service	UPS
36.	Amgen	AMGN
37.	Medtronic	MDT
38.	Morgan Stanley Dean Witter	MWD
39.	Texas Instruments	TXN
40.	Schering-Plough	SGP
41.	American Express	AXP
42.	Federal Home Loan Mortgage	FRE
43.	Disney	DIS
44.	du Pont	DD
45.	Wachovia	WB
46.	Minnesota Mining	MMM
47.	Bank One	ONE
48.	Hewlett Packard	HPQ
49.	Anheuser-Busch	BUD
50.	Merrill Lynch	MER
51.	Goldman Sachs	GS
52.	U.S. Bancorp	USB
53.	Target Corp	TGT
54.	Fifth Third Bancorp	FITB

55.	Walgreen Company	WAG
56.	FleetBoston Financial	FBF
57.	Lowe's Companies	LOW
58.	Gillette	G
59.	Tyco International	TYC
60.	EMC Corp.	EMC
61.	McDonald's	MCD
62.	Sun Microsystems	SUNW
63.	Boeing	BA
64.	Automatic Data Processing	ADP
65.	Washington Mutual	WM
66.	United Technologies	UTX
67.	Baxter International	BAX
68.	QUALCOMM	QCOM
69.	Comcast	CMCSK
70.	Schlumberger	SLB
71.	Kimberly-Clark	KMB
72.	First Data Corp.	FDC
73.	Colgate-Palmolive	CL
74.	AT&T	T
75.	Bank of New York	BK
76.	Alcoa	AA
77.	Cardinal Health	CAH
78.	Electronic Data Systems	EDS
79.	Motorola	MOT
80.	MBNA Corp.	KRB
81.	General Motors	GM
82.	Marsh and McLennan	MMC
83.	Honeywell	HON
84.	Clear Channel Communications	CCU
85.	Duke Energy	DUK
86.	Dow Chemical	DOW
87.	Genentech	DNA
88.	Ford	F

89.	Emerson Electric	EMR
90.	Allstate	ALL
91.	Household International	HI
92.	UnitedHealth Group	UNH
93.	Lockheed Martin	LMT
94.	Applied Materials	AMAT
95.	Kohl's	KSS
96.	HCA Inc.	HCA
97.	Tenet Healthcare	THC
98.	Kraft Foods	KFT
99.	Illinois Tool Works	ITW
100.	International Paper	IP

Since you have command over how you build your personal portfolio, why not start with the big guys?

A logical extension of this strategy is to then add to this large-cap 100-draft list (LC-100) the names of established "foreign" companies that meet the same capitalization requirements and trade actively on U.S. exchanges. In our marketplace, the unit of trading for large foreign companies is represented by American Depository Receipts. ADRs, as they are commonly known, are shares that represent ownership in a defined unit of a foreign company, but they trade on U.S. exchanges in U.S. dollars. Since they technically represent a receipt for foreign shares held by a U.S. bank, they are an efficient way to buy and sell foreign stocks in our currency. ADRs are now available on more than one thousand foreign companies, so they represent a logical way to expand your portfolio into foreign-based franchises.

Think of a group of large cap ADRs as a supplemental draft list that would yield approximately twenty to thirty more great global companies. This list, representing established, world-class corporations, could include, but not be limited to, twenty of the following:

1. Toyota motor	Consumer	Japan	TM
2. Sony Corp	Consumer	Japan	SNE

3. Credit Suisse	Financial	Switzerland	CSR
4. British Petroleum	Energy	Great Britain	BP
5. Glaxo Smithkline	Healthcare	Great Britain	GSK
6. Vodafone Group	Telecomm	Great Britain	VOD
7. Nokia Corp	Telecomm	Finland	NOK
8. Royal Dutch Pet	Energy	Netherlands	RD
9. AstraZeneca	Healthcare	Great Britain	AZN
10. Barclays P.L.C.	Financial	Great Britain	BCS
11. ING Group	Financial	The Netherlands	ING
12. Vivendi Universal	Consumer	France	V
13. Siemens A.G	Industrials	Germany	SI
14. Deutsche Telecom	Telecomm	Germany	DT
15. Unilever	Consumer	Netherlands	UN
16. Daimler Chrysler	Consumer	Germany	DCX
17. Telefonos de Mexico	Telecomm	Mexico	TMX
18. Toshiba	Technology	Japan	n/a
19. Samsung	Technology	Korea	n/a
20. Novartis	Healthcare	Switzerland	NOV
21. Nestle	Consumer	Switzerland	n/a
22. AXA Financial	Financial	France	AXA
23. Diageo	Consumer	Great Britain	DGE
24. Shell Transport	Energy	Netherlands	SC
25. BASF	Conglomerate	Germany	BF

This combined master list, which we can now define as the "global 120," (G-120) represents strong businesses diversified all around the planet. Most of the 120 companies in this master universe are in business in at least 100 different countries. A net positive for you, as a global investor, is that you do not need to be overly concerned with foreign exchange rates or foreign currency exposure. Since most of them actively trade on major U.S. exchanges in U.S. dollars, they offer a consistent level of liquidity and marketability.

What result are we looking for? For one thing, this approach allows you to achieve strong global diversification while staying in your home office. Since the fall of the Berlin Wall over a decade ago, the increasingly global nature of the world's economy has become a fact of life. If you want more proof that we are all part of "one global economy," consider the fact that, in 2001, Coca Cola generated over 55% of its annual revenues outside the United States. (source: Coca-Cola Company Annual Report, 2001) Similar numbers exist for McDonald's, Pepsi, Proctor and Gamble, and many other multinational companies. From Algeria to Argentina, and from South Africa to South Korea, the more than six billion consumers that inhabit the planet have consumption habits that are becoming increasingly similar, and increasingly "Americanized."

To recognize and identify this global 120 (G-120) list is to be well on your way to managing information overload. Imagine that you are a pro football scout, with limited time and limited resources. What if you had the ability to filter the number of college players that you must evaluate before the next draft from 8,000 down to 120? What a relief. In effect, we have just done the same thing, by reducing a massive stock universe down to a meaningful one.

CHAPTER TEN:
THE OFFENSIVE SWEET SPOT

In an effort to find the sweet spot, your offensive equation for success should unite sound investment disciplines in ways that analyze both the broad market and individual stocks from different perspectives. Two popular, yet distinctly different, approaches to the market that have been tested over time are "fundamental analysis" and "technical analysis." Each discipline has its followers on Wall Street, but rather than debate the merits of one over the other, a valid case can be made that a blend of the two distinct investment approaches creates great strength, like an epoxy that bonds only when two different chemicals react with each other.

Would you attempt to play in the club tournament with only your woods and not your irons? No. Would you play a football game by using only running plays and not passing plays? No. Then why should you attempt to make serious investment decisions without considering both fundamental analysis and technical analysis? To use only one of these two distinct disciplines (only fundamental or only technical) is like catching a long pass with only one hand. It can be done, but your odds of success over many attempts are much greater if you always use two hands. While there is no "Holy Grail" when it comes to stock investing, a blend of these two dissimilar disciplines can act like an epoxy that helps you find the "sweet spot" in the market, and can take you a long way down the road to success, confidence, and your own investing highlight reel of experiences.

On the offensive side of the ball, the sweet spot should give you guidance regarding not only what company stock to buy, but also when to buy it. So where do we start? "Fundamental analysis" is a great tool in determining what stocks to buy. "Technical analysis," on the other hand, is a great tool in determining when to buy them, and more importantly, when to sell them. Let's look at the way the benefits of these two ingredients interact together.

The year was . . .?

> **The Soviet Union ceases to exist**
> **Magic Johnson retires from basketball**
> **Twins defeat Braves in World Series**
> **Bret Farve plays in his first season with the Packers**
> **Giants over Bills in Super Bowl**
> **Dow Jones Industrial Average closes at 3,169**

The year was . . . 1991.

Fundamental analysis can assist you in filtering hundreds of bytes of information down to a meaningful set of stocks to consider for investment. For most traditional investors, it is the key ingredient in the recipe they know as the stock selection process. Fans of fundamental analysis learned in business school to follow the numbers, so they believe that the current value of a corporation's stock is heavily dependent on financial variables such as earnings, cash flow, debt to capital, and book value. More importantly, they believe that the projected future value of a stock in a public company should be directly dependent upon changes in these financial characteristics, so for them the search for value always starts with a look at the "fundamentals."

Today these fundamental details about publicly traded companies can be found in numerous places, starting with individual company websites and the annual reports that are posted there. Other information sources include the more traditional independent research services like The Value Line Investment urvey, and Standard and Poor's Stock Reports; or other online sites that track fundamental research on specific companies.

Like a view of the field from high up in the press box, the "top-down" approach to investment analysis is a macro, big-picture approach. It starts with the study of the current and future fundamental health of the overall U.S. economy, so it's a logical starting point in the process of fundamental analysis. This method includes a look at broad economic variables such as gross domestic product, consumer spending, industrial production, and the unemployment rate. As boring as it may sound, this is critical in determining whether or not the outlook for overall U.S. economic growth is favorable or unfavorable, healthy or unhealthy. Is the overall business climate friendly or unfriendly? Is the tide coming in, or going out?

The second step in the top-down, fundamental process considers the prevailing trends and themes in specific sectors of the economy. It is somewhat similar to focusing on one group of players, such as the defensive secondary, rather that the entire team. This step might consider questions such as: which growth sectors of the economy are expected to benefit the most from future social, demographic, and technical trends? Sectors included in contemporary sector analysis might be "healthcare" and "biotechnology," which are expected to benefit from the aging of the baby boomers and a trend towards more healthy lifestyles. Another beneficiary of positive sector trends might be "aerospace and defense," a sector expected to benefit as a result of heightened concerns about terrorism and homeland security. As an additional subset of fundamental analysis, work that considers positive and negative trends in each specific sector of our economy is a critical second layer in the overall stock selection process.

After identifying sectors expected to lead our overall economy, the pure fundamental analyst then digs deeper in an attempt to identify the third level, that is, the individual companies in each positive sector that possess the best prospects for growth. These companies make the first cut, and receive strong consideration for a final "stock selection draft list." In the health and biotechnology sector, individual stocks such as Pfizer and Amgen might be selected. Examples of individual companies in the aerospace and defense sector might include Boeing and Lockheed Martin. (These are strictly hypothetical examples, and this is not an endorsement of any specific company.)

Since it is a common belief among fundamental students of the markets that earnings drive stock prices, these analysts are driven to find truth in the numbers found in financial statements and balance sheets, as well as financial projections that may not yet be as clear to the majority of investors.

If you're a numbers guy (aren't all sports fans numbers guys?), then you will easily connect with the numbers and ratios included in the framework of fundamental analysis. They are the stats that record the track record of a specific company. Examine for a minute the numbers that make up the track record of a great American company like Johnson and Johnson; and the subtle similarity to the numbers that make up the track record of a great American ballplayer like Derek Jeter:

Johnson and Johnson, Financial Statistics

	2001	2000	1999
Earnings Per Share:	$1.84	$1.61	$1.39
Sales: (billions)	$33.0	$29.8	$28.0
Net earnings: (billions)	$5.7	$5.0	$4.3
Return on Equity:	25.4%	26.5%	27.0%

Derek Jeter, Hitting Statistics

	2001	2000	1999
Batting Average:	.311	.339	.349
Runs batted in:	74	73	102
Hits:	191	201	219
Home Runs:	21	15	24

In the land of growth stocks, fundamental analysis should lead you to companies that have the potential to grow earnings over the foreseeable future at rates faster than the growth rate of the overall U.S. economy. It is not uncommon in this discovery process to seek out companies that meet certain benchmarks, somewhat like scouts that seek out wide receivers who can run the forty in less than four and a half seconds, or pitchers who can throw a fastball at least ninety miles per hour. Examples of the many fundamental filters in the world of stock analysis include annual earnings per share growth, return on equity, the ratio of price to sales, and the ratio of price to earnings.

Some of the prominent stock screening websites that you might consider include:

screen.yahoo.com/stocks.html
www.hoovers.com/search/forms/stockscreener
www.quicken.com/investments/stocks/search

It's like the hunt for big game, or the hunt for the great athlete. Time and effort are great tools in the hunt for the trophy, the asset not yet discovered or prized by the other guys in the jungle.

As an example of a stock search based on fundamental variables, consider the following requirements:

1. A publicly traded U.S. company or ADR, (American Depository Receipt)
2. With a capitalization of greater than $22 billion,
3. With earnings per share growth greater than 15% (prior year),
4. With return on equity greater than 15% (prior year).

The search included here was completed in July 2002. From our earlier discussion and definition of the global 120 (G-120) we know that a screen for companies greater than $22 billion in capitalization would include about 120 names. The third filter, the requirement that these companies must have had annual earnings growth last year of at least 15%, reduced the large-cap list of 120 down to twenty names. When we added a fourth variable, such as "return on equity greater than 15%," the draft list was whittled down even further, to only fourteen names.

Sample Fundamental Stock Filter:

Publicly traded U.S. company or American Depository Receipt,	8,000 names
With market capitalization greater than $22 billion,	120 names
With prior year earnings growth greater than 15%,	20 names
With prior year return on equity greater than 15%	14 names

A second way to filter the fundamental strength of the global 120 stock universe is to rely on one of the reputable research services. An example would be the Value Line Investment Survey, an independent service that ranks stocks based on a 1 through 5 timeliness ranking system. One possible approach would be to consider stocks from our G-120 subset that are rated 1 or 2 by the Value Line service. At any given time, based on the defined rating system developed by the Value Line Investment Survey, these companies, rated 1 or 2, are projected to be fundamentally stronger, and more timely for purchase, than the average U.S. stock.

At the time of this writing, twenty-nine names from the global 120 list made the cut as companies rated either 1 or 2 by Value Line. They qualify for the next level of analysis, but for now we will put this number and this method of defining fundamentally sound companies aside, knowing that we will come back to it shortly.

Much like the players named to an all-star team, the names that remain as a result of these exercises must be doing something right, so they are worthy of consideration to start the game. However, just as players have career years, and then less-than-career years, the names on this roster will come and go because of the heavy dependence on recent performance. As it says in the fine print, any analysis of this type is "subject to change without notice." Our purpose here is to simply provide an example of the fundamental filtering included in the first half of the "dual analysis" system.

So, how do we get to the sweet spot of "dual analysis"? Consider this logic: The composite force of all "fundamental" reports, analysis, and thinking about a stock leads to market activity, which leads to price and volume changes, which is recorded as the discipline known as "technical" analysis. There you go. We made it. That's our next move.

CHAPTER ELEVEN:
THE OTHER HALF OF DUAL ANALYSIS

The second element in the search for the sweet spot of dual analysis is "technical analysis," a discipline that originated over 100 years ago with a "figuring" approach used by Charles Dow (Dow Theory, Dow Jones Industrial Average). His methods have evolved into a logical way of recording price and volume movements, and the constant struggle that exists in the stock market between the forces of supply and demand. With all the concern in the marketplace recently regarding accounting principles and corporate reform, it is interesting to note that the technical method of tracking stock movements grew in popularity in the early 1900s, a time when it was much harder to get consistent, accurate financial (fundamental) information directly from domestic companies.

The basis for technical analysis involves the charting of historic and current price and volume levels. For many of its followers, it is one means of remaining unemotional in an emotional auction marketplace, because the premise of technical analysis is that a graphic record of price and volume movements creates an objective, unbiased signal regarding the overall health of a common stock. Supply and demand, like a tug of war between buyers and sellers, is recorded in various graphic ways that give a picture of the emotional reality of the marketplace. For many followers, technical methods actually do more than other variables to record the net optimism or net pessimism regarding a particular asset. For that reason, technical analysis is in many ways a great "interpreter" of the foreign language known as "market sentiment."

If a numerical "high-low-close" quote out of the Wall Street Journal is a black and white TV picture, then a technical analysis graph of a stock is a color high-definition TV picture. It has more value than a few numbers because it records a high-resolution picture of the past and present sentiment and psychology that is embedded in the price levels of a specific stock or a specific index.

The year was . . .?

Kentucky over Duke for NCAA basketball title

Yankees win World Series over L.A. Dodgers

Sony introduces the Walkman, the first portable stereo

Affirmed wins the Kentucky Derby

Cowboys over Broncos in Super Bowl

Dow Jones Industrial Average closes the year at 805

The year was . . . 1978.

One overriding theme of technical analysis is that players change and price levels change, but the basic nature of the market never changes. This leads to the conclusion that a graphic picture of the current relative price level of a stock is a true representation of all of the current "fundamental" thinking about that stock (note the link between fundamental and technical). All the analysis from hundreds of pages of data and opinions from research reports, annual reports, and cyberspace information sources becomes a part of the supply versus demand tug-of-war that is represented by the current technical picture of that stock. To look at it another way, if every "player-investor" in a particular stock has put his money where his mind is, that sentiment and that action is reflected in the composite picture that we know as the current quote. In the end, the ultimate truth in any marketplace is found in one place, and that's the last trade (price level). That fact is not necessarily good or evil, it is just one of the wonderful realities of a free marketplace.

You can observe a lot by just watching.

Yogi Berra
Philosopher, Ballplayer

From one perspective, the market is a moving bull's-eye that records the constant battle between the supply of shares outstanding and the demand for those shares. Charts, to many followers of technical analysis, provide a legitimate way of recording an ever-evolving balance of power. Imbalances and inefficiencies lead to shifts in price trends and price levels, which become the "stat sheets" for the markets that we know as charts and graphs.

A key principal of the technical approach to investing is that a trend develops and continues for a reasonable period of time, until it is interrupted by some counterforce that disrupts that trend. In a less than perfect scientific comparison to the laws of physics, technical analysis suggests that a body in motion tends to stay in motion, along a path of least resistance, until some force changes its path. That force is usually the net flow of money, which is a result of the net demand for the shares. To the technician, a prevailing trend is a path of least resistance, and is one of the most important pieces of information on the stat sheet. A prevailing trend might last for a week, or a year, or even longer, but it will not change until some significant change occurs in the forces of supply or demand.

Any specific stock chart represents a composite picture of all of the past and present thinking that has become the financial DNA of that stock. Many factors—political, social, psychological, and economic—that influence the asset value are reflected in the current price.

In price there is knowledge.

Motto of The Professional
Technical Analysis Association

To the perceptive student, price and volume levels provide constant clues (pictures) regarding the impact of Econ 101. These indicators represent the net optimism or the net pessimism of all the players who are in the game. Once a prevailing trend becomes either optimistic or pessimistic, it is likely to continue along that basic path of least resistance in the near term. To the market technician, the ability to recognize these price and volume trends in a dynamic marketplace is a critical element of not only the stock selection process, but also the stock deletion process. The trend can become an old friend, but in order to go with it, you must first recognize it.

Like an ocean current, prices are always in motion in an adjustment process that seeks an equilibrium price, pauses, and then seeks a new equilibrium price. For that reason, "technical analysis" is not as much about forecasting the future as it is about recognizing signals in the present. If price trends can be analyzed in the "now," they can become road signs that can lead us to a specific course of action in the market right "now." Technical analysis uses relationships found in past dynamics of the market to measure the current dynamics of the market, based on the charting of real market data. When confirming signals exist, as a result of a similarity to past stock price movements, those signals provide an additional layer of investor self-confidence, which prodives more justification for the use of the technical analysis discipline.

There is no present or future, only the past repeating itself

Anonymous

Some academics argue that fundamental analysis and technical analysis are opposing forces, like two great religions or political parties. Others, including this writer, prefer to think of these two disciplines as strong allies in the overall stock selection process. Technical analysis is not some "tea leaves" method of fortune telling. The interactive characteristic of the two disciplines comes into focus when you admit that "technical analysis" represents the composite details of all of the recent and current "fundamental analysis" surrounding a specific investment. Once you accept that point of view, the two disciplines interact more closely than most business professors would prefer to admit. We all know that it is better to attempt to catch a long pass with two hands rather than with one hand. Sure, you can do it with one hand or the other, but you improve your odds of success if you use both. The same thing rings true for the use of both fundamental and technical analysis.

One of the key features of technical analysis is the definition of "moving average" price lines, which register an arithmetic average of a stock's closing price over a specific period of time, such as the most recent fifty days, 100 days, or 200 days. A moving average price line with an inclining slope is obviously indicative of an average price level that is rising, which is a signal that demand for that stock is increasing. Since an up-trend is an indication that demand is overtaking supply, it can signal a general price increase, and an obvious benefit to bullish shareholders. You may ask, "where is the demand coming from? Is it coming from mutual funds, foreign investors, individual investors, or institutional investors?" No one knows, and a good technical analyst does not even spend time attempting to answer that question. In his mind, the reason for the up-trend is not important. The critical factor is to recognize the up-trend, analyze it, and then take constructive action in order to ride the positive wave of demand.

See it, read it, hit it.

Ted Williams
Baseball Legend

Conversely, a moving average price line with a declining slope is an indication that something negative is below the surface, and that supply in overtaking demand. This negative trend may be the result of insider selling, institutional selling, mutual fund redemptions, all of the above, or none of the above. Worrying about answers to the questions "who" or "why" is a waste of time to the technical analyst. The important thing is to recognize the downtrend, monitor it, and take the appropriate action based upon the technical signal of a specific market. "See it, read it, hit it," in the words of the great Ted Williams.

Although stock trends are not a perfect indicator, they are somewhat like tracking a hitter in a groove, or a hitter in a slump. Baseball managers who go with recent hitting stats are simply focusing on recent trends, as in the case of a manager who makes a pitch-hitter selection based on this month's stats. It is commonly believed that a pure technical analyst should be able to make a rational decision regarding the trend of a specific stock without even knowing the name of the company. The picture (graph) tells the story, and is the most important piece of the puzzle.

Through accessing various websites and technical analysis services, you can track simple moving averages based upon any period of time, ranging from as little as ten days to as long as 200 days or more. Financial publications, as well as many professional investors, have a tendency to focus on the 200-day moving average, and it is generally considered to be one of the more meaningful moving average indicators. In the volatile markets of recent years, the 200-day moving average is monitored by more investors on both sides of Wall Street than ever before. For that reason, a case can be made that the relationship of the stock's current price to the 200-day moving average is the single most important club in the technical analyst's golf bag. Stated another way, it would probably be the last technical indicator that most VSIs (veteran stock investors) would give up if they were forced to surrender their technical tools.

In using technical analysis to gauge the strength of the market, it is wise to first consider the moving average of the major market indices, such as the S&P 500 Equity Index. Since you're a football fan, one way to do this is to think of the 200-day moving average of the S&P 500 much like the fifty-yard line, or the equilibrium point, on the playing field.

If you were the offensive coordinator for a team that took over possession of the football, you would naturally favor your position and take a more aggressive offensive approach if you gained possession in the other team's territory versus your own territory. In a comparative way, an S&P 500 Index level above its moving average indicates better field position than one that is priced significantly below its 200-day moving average.

On the other hand, if the overall market reading places the ball on your own thirty-yard line (that is, below the fifty-yard line), this is a general signal of market weakness, and it warrants a more conservative approach to the overall market. This general signal exists when the S&P 500 Index reading is below it's 200-day moving average.

> *There are times when your money should be waiting on the sidelines in cash. Time is not money. Time is time, and money is money.*
>
> ***Jesse Livermore***
> ***Legendary Investor***

Performance studies suggest that as much as 65% to 75% of an individual stock's performance can be attributed to the overall performance of the general market, plus the performance of that stock's specific sector. For that reason alone, it is critical to get a reading on the health of the overall market and specific sectors before charging out and buying any individual stock.

If you take over the ball on the opponent's thirty-yard line, you have a reasonable probability of scoring some points on that possession, and you can take a more aggressive approach to the plays that you call. The significance of your position on the field should never be taken lightly, in football or in the free market.

In order to further explore how your market play selection should be influenced by your field position, compare the current relationship of the S&P 500 Index to its 200-day moving average. Your overall offensive game plan should start with three distinct market situations, based on this primary technical relationship. Consider the classic matrix that follows:

CASE 1.) If the S&P 500 Index is greater than 2% above the 200-

day moving average of the S&P 500 Index, define this as having a green light. Define this as "Attack" mode. Since this represents the most positive of the three total market signals, the decisions you make should be based on the moderate to aggressive section of your playbook. In football terms compare this signal to having possession of the football inside the opponent's thirty-yard line.

"GREEN LIGHT"
Courtesy of stockcharts.com
used with permission

Recall that any complete approach to technical analysis first considers the signal of the overall market (S&P 500 Index), and then considers the signal of a specific stock. The overriding rule is that the "signal" is the most important variable, whether analyzing one big market or one small stock.

You will note that the graphs displayed in this section detail three distinct relationships (Cases I,II, and III), based on a current reading of three individual stocks. Our overriding purpose is to give clarity to the characteristics of these three distinct market situations. Thus, even though we exhibit graphs of specific stocks, the true value of the exercise lies in always making the same master reading of the relationship between the "price" (level) and the "200-day moving average of the price," regardless of whether you are viewing one specific stock, or the S&P 500 Index.

Gillette Co (G) NYSE © StockCharts.com

CASE 2.) "YELLOW LIGHT"
Courtesy of stockcharts.com
used with permission

CASE 2.) If the 200-day moving average of the S&P 500 Index is in a range between 2% above to 2% below the S&P 500 Index, define this as having a yellow light, and as "Balance" mode. This represents a neutral reading of the total market, so decisions when the market gives this signal should be based on a moderate section of the playbook until the market breaks out of this range (either positively or negatively). Compare this situation to slack tide, a time when the market has no clear trend. Leaders and laggards will emerge, but it is generally smart to let more time pass before getting overly bullish or overly bearish. As a football fan, compare this to having possession of the ball between the forty- yard lines. Things could be better, but things could also be a lot worse.

International Paper Co (IP) NYSE © StockCharts.com

CASE 3.)

"RED LIGHT"
Courtesy of stockcharts.com
used with permission

CASE 3.) In this case, the S&P 500 Index is greater than 2% below the 200-day moving average of the S&P 500 Index. Define this as having a red light, and as the "Control" zone. This technical situation represents the most negative of the three readings of the overall market, so decisions you make should be based on the most conservative section of your playbook, and caution should prevail until the signals of the market strengthen. Compare this to having possession of the ball, but with field position inside your own thirty-yard line.

Matrix: Relationship of "Price" to "200-Day Moving Average of Price"

1. Price greater than 2% above "moving average"	Attack Zone	Green Light
2. Price from 2% above to 2% below "moving avg"	Balance Zone	Yellow Light
3. Price greater than 2% below "moving average"	Control Zone	Red Light

Always realize that as the journey continues, the landscape and the road signs will change. In fact, the only thing we know for sure is that your position relative to that of your opponent will change. This is one of the great mysteries, and at the same time one of the great opportunities, of the market. Nevertheless, the first step in determining what section of the plan to use is to clearly define what zone the overall market is in. You then know whether to emphasize attack mode, balance mode, or control mode.

It is crucial to get a feel for where you are on the field, and how your opponent (the market) is setup. After you know where you are on the field, you can then revisit the draft list of fundamentally strong companies that we identified earlier through the fundamental filter methods. These companies have "potential," so now you can use the second half of dual analysis to determine the starting players for an all-pro portfolio.

We complete this draft, which in this case is the process of portfolio stock selection, through sweat equity, with a detailed review of the current charts of our previously selected, fundamentally sound companies in order to compare the relationship of the fifty-day moving average, the 200-day moving average, and the current price of each stock. Just as the offensive coordinator reviews game films to gain a better understanding of individual player tendencies, we now review these relationships in order to gain a better understanding of individual stock tendencies.

A good place to start is by using one of the many technical charting services or websites. Possible sources of this information for individual stocks include:

www.bigcharts.com
www.cbsmarketwatch.com
www.bloomberg.com
www.decisionpoint.com
www.investors.com
www.stockcharts.com

The fifty-day moving average is a shorter-term gauge of a stock's performance, much like a hitters stats over the past twenty games. It signals streaks and slumps in the recent price trends of a stock. On the other hand, the 200-day moving average is a longer-term indicator of accumulation (increasing demand) or distribution (decreasing demand), and is more comparable to hitter's stats over an entire season.

The relationship of these three variables, (current price, fifty-day moving average, and 200-day moving average), is a key signal of the relative strength or weakness of the stock. We call this simple exercise "stacking," because by reviewing a current graph of each previously identified stock, you can then determine the simple mathematical relationship of these three variables. The way that they are "stacked" relative to each other can lead to only one of the following six possibilities:

	STACKING FORMATION	SIGNAL
I	1. 200-day moving average 2. Fifty-day moving average 3. current price	very weak
II	1. Fifty-day moving average 2. 200-day moving average 3. current price	very weak
III	1. 200-day moving average 2. current price 3. Fifty-day moving average	weak

IV	1. Fifty-day moving average 2. current price 3. 200-day moving average	weak
V	1. Fifty-day moving average 2. current price 3. 200-day moving average	strong
VI	1. current price 2. Fifty-day moving average 3. 200-day moving average	very strong

An example of Formation VI, a pattern that exhibits a high degree of technical strength, is shown below in the chart of Apollo Group, Inc.

Apollo Grp., Inc. (APOL) NNM © StockCharts.com

Formation VI
Courtesy of stockcharts.com
used with permission

Caveat: it is best to consider stocks rated "strong" and "very strong" that are still trading within 5% of the 200-day moving average. If the current price is more than 5% above the 200-day, the stock may be extended too far to chase, and may have to consolidate in the short run. Keep these stocks under consideration for purchase, but respect the fact that the best candidates to own are those FormationV and VI stocks that are above the 200-day, but still within 5% of it.

Through the use of the dual analysis (fundamental and technical) discussed in this section, you now have the tools to screen a spreadsheet filled with over 120 names down to a handful of just a few. After this type of exercise, it is not unusual to find that less than ten stocks make the cut as the strongest buy candidates. These ten or so, the best of the breed, are set to become the first-round draft picks for your portfolio (see below).

This hypothetical exercise is an example of a stock selection process that you can apply to your own portfolio. In any case, it has hopefully served a purpose by making you more aware of a defined way to use technical and fundamental analysis in concert with each other in the ways of a VSI.

Sample Dual Analysis Stock Filter:

Publicly traded U.S. company or
American Depository Receipt, ...8,000 names
With market capitalization
greater than $22 billion, ...120 names
With prior year earnings
growth greater than 15%, .20 names
With prior year return on
equity greater than 15%, ...14 names
With a "strong" or "very strong"
technical signal . . . . .8 names

Let's revisit a couple of additional points that are very important to the portfolio process. We now respect the importance of protective sell-stop orders, with the red flag at minus 9% as a constant entry in our playbook. Now that we have reviewed the merits of technical analysis, there is another rule dependent on the relationship of current market price and the 200-day moving average that should be respected. It is easy to monitor since it is based on closing daily prices. If one of your stocks slips to a closing price more than 1% below its 200-day moving average, this is an overriding signal of weakness that should lead to major defensive action anytime it shows up on your radar screen.

If this defined closing price break occurs, sell the position, sell part of the position, place it on your "exit on a bounce within the next two days" list, but do something. Respect this sign that weakness is overtaking strength. While no signal is correct 100% of the time, and sometimes you will get whip-sawed by a volatile market, this is one sign that can help you avoid tons of trouble. Obey it. Follow it. Act on it.

Also, at various points along the way, we have discussed the strategy of building a portfolio in a bull market that includes at least twenty to twenty-five names. We do that in order to keep boundaries on the market risk inherent in any portfolio. To take this boundary analogy one step further, I recommend that you set limits on your percentage exposure from any specific company so that an adverse event will not take you out of the game. Call it a simple "boundary system." If you are forced out of bounds, you have no chance of losing more ground on that play. Similarly, you should limit the dollar exposure associated with any individual stock to 6% or less. That way you establish white chalk-lines to take you out of bounds and out of trouble. At a maximum 6% position, even if you are forced out of bounds (out of a stock position) at a loss of 9% to 10%, you limit the mathematical risk to your total portfolio to less than 1%. Consider the following example in a $100,000 portfolio:

6% long position equals $6,000
$6,000 at 10% sell-stop level equals $600 loss
$600 equals .6% (six-tenths of 1% of a $100,000 portfolio)

In this example, setting boundaries keeps you actively in the game, but at the same time controls downside risk. One play that takes you out of bounds will not take you out of the game. As a disciplined investor, you know by now that you always set these boundaries sooner rather than later, at the time play begins, and at the time you buy the stock.

After you have filtered your G-120 draft list down to the five, or ten, or fifteen first round picks that you would consider for your portfolio, the next step is to create an offensive game plan built around these select companies that can give you an edge early in the game. This game plan should be simple, effective and based upon tested strategies that you have confidence in. Come on. Let's take a look.

CHAPTER TWELVE:

THE "ELEVATOR OFFENSE"

Imagine that several years ago in the late 1990's, you were the general manager of the St. Louis Rams. You sign a young, untested quarterback with strong physical tools by the name of Warner. The problem is that he had a very average college career, and he even had played in the arena football league. A sound business decision based upon what you knew at that time was to sign him for a reasonably low salary, invest a moderate amount of money in him, and then give him some time to play out as an investment.

That type of thing happens all the time in sports. The initial investment in the player is small, the risk of a bust is limited, and the potential upside is virtually unlimited. Admittedly, the player in this case was Kurt Warner, but at the time he first signed with the Rams, few thought that he would turn out to be one of the great football "finds" of the past decade.

The year was . . .?

Oilers over Flyers for Stanley Cup
Nintendo entertainment system is introduced
Joe Namath and O.J. Simpson are inducted into the NFL Hall of Fame
Lakers over Celtics for NBA title
San Francisco over Miami in Super Bowl
Dow Jones Industrial Average closes at 1,547

The year was . . . 1985.

Limited-risk strategies like the Kurt Warner example are executed all the time by great sports franchises. Front office personnel analyze the potential upside of an untested player, they make a small initial investment in him, and then they monitor him while he is given a chance to prove himself. Only later do they make a decision to place more of their total capital on this particular player. There is a solid "scaling in" investment process, based upon the same logic, that we call the "elevator offense." Let's take a look.

Specifically, a logical, strategic way to build a desired total number of shares in a stock is to scale into it in three phases, based on the following formula:

Assume that "company A" makes your final draft list based upon your most recent dual analysis. You decide to place as much as 6% of your total portfolio value into "company A." For purposes of this example, we will consider your total portfolio value to be $100,000.

How does the "scaling in" process play out? You buy a 2% position of your total portfolio value in company A. This $2,000 commitment represents one-third of the 6% total investment that you eventually want to own in company A.

If company A goes down 9%, your defense takes the field, and your previously defined sell-stop discipline takes you out of the position. You sell at a small, manageable loss, and by taking action you "kill a loser." The action of the game goes against you, so your reaction is to recognize reality and sell out of your position. This event is comparable to a game situation where a key player gets injured. It is a setback, but it is just a part of the game. The injured player leaves the game, your team momentum stalls for the moment, but the game goes on, and the overall offensive game plan stays intact.

On the other hand, if company A goes up 5%, at that point no one knows if it is a fake-out or a breakout. You don't need to answer that question yet, since only time and the market will tell you, anyway. What do you do? As a disciplined growth investor, you take action by investing another one-third of your desired final investment in that specific stock position ($2,000 or 2% more of your total portfolio value is added to Company A). You also adjust your protective sell order on the entire position to seven percent below x, your first cost.

If company A goes up another 5% from this second level, you add the final one-third of your desired position (2% of total portfolio value). At this point you have attained your original goal of 6%, or $6,000 of your total portfolio, invested in company A. You again adjust your protective sell order on the entire position to five percent below x, your first cost.

1	2	3
		THIRD BUY “X” PLUS 10%
	SECOND BUY “X” PLUS 5%	
RST BUY PRICE “X”		
” MINUS 9% LL-STOP ALL SHARES	“X” MINUS 7% SELL-STOP ALL SHARES	“X” MINUS 5% SELL-STOP ALL SHARES

“ELEVATOR OFFENSE”

Although it goes against human nature to pay up for anything, this “elevator offense,” defined as adding to stock positions only if they prove themselves by going up in price, is systematic, logical, and unemotional. It compares to a sports franchise that invests in a player, monitors his progress or lack of progress, and then makes a second business decision regarding whether to invest more in him or not.

Many VSIs will tell you that professionals average up, while amateurs average down. Admittedly, this is inconsistent with the mindset of most novice investors, who have been preconditioned to buy at the best price, which to them often means the most discounted price. The fact is that to average up, by buying more of a stock only after it goes up from your initial buy point, is not a bad thing to do. What if you were a businessman who owned a Kentucky thoroughbred farm? You would start each racing season with a stable of yearlings, and as a savvy horse guy, you would add investment dollars to the training and development of the colts that proved themselves as they developed into two-year-olds. Regrettably, you would have to cut your investment in the two-year-olds that didn't show well; but you would nurture your winners, and add money to support them. You would not be afraid to invest more in the training and development of your strongest horses, which represent your strongest assets. Likewise, don't be afraid to invest more in your strongest stocks, which represent your strongest portfolio assets.

This idea of paying up to buy more of anything may not be in your mental makeup right now, but over time you should make it a common part of your offensive strategy. From this minute on, work on getting over the "perfection obsession." Rather than focusing on perfect execution, focus on the overall process, let the execution take care of itself, and remain confident that you can be wildly successful as an investor with less than perfect execution. Recognize the reality that it's better to have a simple playbook and strong execution, rather than a complex playbook and weak execution.

1	2	3
		THIRD BUY $110
	SECOND BUY $105	
FIRST BUY $100		
$91 SELL-STOP ALL SHARES	$93 SELL-STOP ALL SHARES	$95 SELL-STOP ALL SHARES

"ELEVATOR OFFENSE" $100 STOCK

By constantly remaining mindful of this elevator-offense matrix, what do you accomplish? By maintaining a kill it or feed it approach to your portfolio, what do you accomplish? You cut your losers like bad draft picks. They bring you no gain, but no significant pain, either. The positive side of the probability spectrum is equally important, because you add to and nurture your winners, the companies that prove themselves by performing positively. You give them an opportunity to generate profits and put some points on the board for your offense. With this strategy, your stronger stock selections become a greater percentage of your total portfolio, and more dollars remain invested in your better performing ideas, much like the top-line players on a baseball team. After all, a proven pitcher like Roger Clemens has more of George Steinbrenner's money backing him than an unproven second-year guy in the minor leagues. Fewer dollars remain invested in the ideas that have yet to prove themselves, which is just good business.

Two hundred years ago, an Italian economist named Pareto developed a theory regarding the relationship between producers and output. In simple street terminology, his thinking is commonly known as the 80/20 rule, signaling that 80% of our results come from 20% of our effort. This rule has significance for the VSI, because it is not unreasonable to expect that as much as 80% of your profits may come from only 20% of your stock selections. This adaptation of Pareto's Principle is worth noting because it again emphasizes the reality that you don't have to be even close to perfect regarding your initial stock picks. If you stay with this offensive discipline, and manage the portfolio like a pool of players, you lessen the chances of a portfolio blowup. One bad offensive series of plays will not crush you. One punch will not knock you out. Sure, you will have losers, winners, and those that get stuck in between. But over an extended market cycle, you will give your winners opportunities to break loose and perform in ways that make some significant money for the team.

Just as winter follows autumn, and just as spring training follows the Super Bowl, market downturns follow market upturns. It is such a simple statement, but that, more than any other, is the reason why it is mandatory that your offensive game plan include ways of protecting unrealized paper profits that build up in your portfolio. If you don't have a plan for this positive contingency, paper profits can slip away like sand on the beach, never to be seen again.

The following formula is one example of a sound strategy that you can use to harvest some of the gains that develop in your portfolio. Finally, we get to talk about gains. It's about time, right?

Harvest rule #1: Always be aware of the average cost per share of each of your stock positions. This can be accomplished with a sophisticated spreadsheet, or with a legal pad and a hand-held calculator. If the total value of any one stock position grows to a 25% profit above your first buy price, (X), sell one-third of your shares in that specific stock. Adjust your open sell-stop order on the remaining shares to the original share cost (X), plus 6%.

Harvest Rule #2: If the total value of any one specific stock position grows to a 50% profit above your average cost, sell the second third, based on the greatest number of shares that you held in that stock. Leave your open sell-stop order on the remaining shares (The math of this matrix is shown below.) Note that after this profitable chain of events, this strategy incorporates keeping the final one-third of your original shares, but with a relaxed open sell-stop discipline that helps insure against loss of your original investment. You, as a long-term growth investor, retain the upside potential of shares that might continue to grow into a hall-of-famer, but you have also generated a very respectable return on the first two-thirds of your total investment position.

1	2	3	4	5
				"X" PLUS 50% SELL 1/3
			"X" PLUS 25% SELL 1/3	
		"X" PLUS 10% BUY 1/3		
	"X" PLUS 5% BUY 1/3			
X" BUY 1/3				
X" MINUS 9% TOP	"X" MINUS 7% STOP	"X" MINUS 5% STOP	"X" PLUS 6% STOP	"X" PLUS 6% STOP

"ELEVATOR OFFENSE" — "HARVEST" MATRIX

Consider the guy who owns an orange grove in Florida. There are times when he harvests some of his crop. He sells oranges on the open market, and by doing so, returns some cash to his orange grove business, because his objective is not to hoard oranges, but rather to run a profitable ongoing business, right? He maintains the core foundation of his business, represented by the land and the orange grove, but he systematically harvests some of his crop, harvests some profits, and scores some points for the home team. As a prudent stock investor, there are times when you must pull the trigger and do the same thing. It's your right as a capitalist to do so.

> *For everything there is a season, and a time for every matter under heaven . . . a time to plant, and a time to reap.*
>
> ***Ecclesiastes 3: 1-2***
>
> ***Bible, Revised Standard Version***

The formula for harvesting stock gains that we outlined above is analogous to harvesting a crop, or harvesting a partial profit from a business enterprise. When you are fortunate enough to select a stock that performs like a racing champion, this harvesting formula plan forces you to secure a profit on the first two-thirds of your position. Above all, by implementing this plan, you retain an ownership position in the final one-third of your shares, and you retain all the out-of-the-park, homerun potential of that company if it turns into a mega-performer like a Microsoft or a Home Depot. Analogous to retaining the rights to a powerful college or foreign amateur player, you still hold the rights to the future success of the final one-third of your original total shares. At this point, if you adjust your sell-stop order on this final position to first cost (x) plus 6%, you can stand a great deal of variance in a volatile market, and still protect your original investment against loss.

Go ahead and admit it. Imperfection is not a bad thing. Imperfection is not your enemy. In the end, 90% of the time that you make a sell decision, you will either be too early or too late. Accept the fact that you can miss the center of the target and still be very successful. If you wait for "perfection" in the market, you will miss out on more opportunities than you can imagine, and you may just drive yourself batty in the process. Forget perfect, knowing that even if you miss the first 20% of the profit on a stock, and you miss the last 20%, you can still capture the middle 60%.

In the past fifty years, approximately 300 World Series games have been played. Out of all of those games, there was only one pitcher who threw a perfect game. Don Larsen, in the 1956 game between his Yankees and the Brooklyn Dodgers, is the only guy to achieve perfection at the World Series level. One perfect game out of 300 represents less than one half of 1%. In point of fact, there have been only sixteen perfect games thrown in the modern history of the major leagues. That number, when compared to the thousands of games played, is microscopic. Don't worry about perfection, because it's probably overrated, anyway.

CHAPTER THIRTEEN:
THE BEST TIME TO INVEST

But when is the best time to invest a least "some" of your long-term money in the stock market? How about "now." How about "when you have it." History proves that if your objectives include growing your portfolio value profitably over time, doing nothing may actually be a very bad thing to do.

When a fool has made up his mind, the market has gone by.

Spanish proverb

The math backs up my point. When you consider that the S & P 500 Equity Index measured approximately "10" in 1942, and measured above "1000" in 2002, the undeniable truth of capitalistic compounding is revealed to you. Yes, that is a sixty-year period, but these numbers also represent an average annual rate of return of greater than 10%. In fact, Ibbotson Associates, one of the most respected research firms in the industry, provides the following detail regarding the average annual return of various investments over long windows of time:

Period: 1926 through 2001:	
Large Company U.S. Stocks	10.7% average annual return
U.S. Treasury Bonds	5.3% average annual return
U.S. Treasury Bills	3.8% average annual return
source: Ibbotson Associates	

The question is often asked, is it a bull market or a bear market? We hear it from the talking TV heads all the time. If you can back away from the daily noise and take a long-term perspective, you can make a case that it's always a bull market. The pace of the market moves like an Indy car race—green light, fast pace, pitstop, refuel, race, yellow light, green light, fast pace. The "great race" continues at varying rates of speed, includes breaks and interruptions, but it continues, just as the growth in the profits of great companies continues. In some ways, a case can be made that it's always a bull market.

As detailed previously, this is not to suggest that every investor should remain 100% invested in stocks at all times. It is still important to read the road signs and the flags that signal the condition of the track in this race we call investing. As a free market capitalist, I will own common stocks until the day I die; sometimes more, sometimes less. Sometimes I will own stocks at a level that represents 50% of my liquid net worth, and sometimes I will own stocks at a level that represents 90% of my liquid net worth. I will do this, not because I am a genius, but because I have great faith in the wind at my back that is represented by the long-term performance record of large company stocks.

The year was . . .?

Braves over Indians in World Series
Forrest Gump wins Academy Award for Best Picture
Oklahoma City bombing
Cal Ripken Jr. sets MLB record of 2131 consecutive games
Houston over Orlando for NBA title
Dow Jones Industrial Average crosses 5,000 for first time and closes at 5,117

The year was . . . 1995.

Let's explore the power of time and the history of another key composite measure of stock values, the Dow Jones Industrial Average. Although the makeup of this average has changed over the past fifty years, it is a weighted-average value of thirty of the most dominant companies in America, and as such, it is the most recognized picture of the U.S. market. For reference, note that the Dow Jones Industrial Average traded above the 10,000 level in 2002. Now go back in your memory bank to a significant year in your life, such as the year you were born, or the year you graduated from high school. If you graduated from high school in 1996, the Dow Jones closed out that year at 6,448. If you graduated in 1986, the Dow closed that year at 1,896. If you were born in 1975, the Dow closed that year at 852. Consider:

Year	Event in your life?	Closing value: DJIA
1960	your birth	616
1970	your birth	839
1975	your graduation	852
1980	your birth	964
1982	your graduation	1,047
1984	your graduation	1,212
1986	your graduation	1,896
1988	your graduation	2,169
1990	your wedding	2,634
1992	birth of your child	3,301
1994	your wedding	3,834
1996	birth of your child	6,448
1998	your wedding	9,181
2000	your graduation	10,787

Powerful stuff. Time and the miracle of capitalistic compounding should never be forgotten, even though issues and uncertainties almost always seem to cloud the short-term view.

What about bonds, you ask? In general, if you are seeking superior growth of your net worth over time, you can be a fan of Barry, but don't be a fan of Bonds.

Over the past few years, a great baseball record has been challenged several times. Any good baseball fan knows that the Babe hit sixty in 1927, Maris hit sixty-one in 1961, and McGwire hit seventy in 1998. Then, in 2001, at the age of 37, a guy named Barry Bonds eclipsed every player to ever play the game by hitting seventy-three home runs in one season.

Sure, Barry Bonds is a complete player who has been compared to other greats like Willie Mays and Roberto Clemente. My purpose here is not to demean him in any way. The point is that, in some ways, "bonds" as a financial asset are an inferior investment for the growth investor.

A bond is a debt instrument, typically an agreement by one party to pay a stated rate of interest to a second party over some fixed period of time, and then repay the original principal to the second party at a fixed maturity date. Bonds are typically issued by governments, corporations, or municipalities. It is important to note what they are and what they are not. They represent a loan from one party to another. They do not represent equity ownership in anything. Bonds, in the financial world, represent "to loan" versus "to own," and debt versus equity.

While bonds may certainly have a place in portfolios that require current income, history shows that the long-term growth investor will be better served over time by considering ownership in great companies that issue common stock to the public.

Consider why. Let's say that a major corporation like General Electric issues both corporate bonds and corporate stock to the public, and let's compare the benefits to the guy who buys the bonds instead of the stock. Yes, he can generally plan on receiving a fixed cash flow from his investment, plus the return of his original investment at the maturity date of the bonds. But, along the way, what if GE was to have an outstanding year where earnings and profits beat all previous projections? Would bondholders receive any incremental benefit? No. They would not participate in the upside rewards of the business, because even then, they would receive only the same fixed annual rate of interest that was originally promised to them. On the other hand, the owner of GE common stock could potentially benefit from improved business conditions, an improved perception of GE stock in the marketplace, and an enhanced stock value.

Real wealth can come to those who own stock in great business franchises, take on measurable risk, and monitor that risk. The icons of the American marketplace, including Gates, Trump, Walton, and Buffet are living proof. It is common knowledge that these guys built their financial empires through equity ownership in their companies. On the other hand, it is difficult, if not impossible, to name a significant investor who achieved his financial status by owning bonds, or by loaning money at some fixed rate. If your long-term objectives include growth of capital and accumulation of wealth, stay in the equity game. After all, you have to be "in it" to "win it."

Treasury Bonds and Money Market Funds Do Not Rally

Do you remember "the drive" directed by John Elway against the Cleveland browns in the final two minutes of the 1987 AFC Championship game? Amazing. Ninety-eight yards. Fans in Cleveland and Denver sure remember it. Great warriors like Elway, Montana, Marino, and Staubach all had an uncanny ability to rally from a deficit in ways that stand the test of time. For most of us, the stories actually get better with age.

"Cash," on the other hand, does not rally. Cash, which over the past twenty years has become synonymous with money market funds, represents money parked in short term financial instruments such as treasury bills, commercial paper, and certificates of deposit. All major mutual fund companies and brokerage firms offer money market funds that give investors the equivalent of a short-term cash account. While these money market funds are very liquid and very safe, they pay floating, variable rates of return directly related to short-term U.S. interest rates. Over the five-year period ending in 2002, these annual rates ranged from approximately 1.5% to 6.5%. In fact, Ibbotson Associates reports that the average annual return on U.S. Treasury Bills for the entire period from 1926 through 2001 was only 3.8%.

That historical return rate is an obvious problem for the growth investor who is attempting to accumulate wealth. Even at a rate of 4%, it takes eighteen years for money to double in value, and that fact doesn't even make any allowance for the impact of taxes. Treasury bills don't represent any equity ownership in anything, because they simply represent money loaned to the government for a fixed rate of interest. Somewhat like a third string quarterback carrying a clipboard on the sideline, cash has no major chance of rallying and putting points on the board. If you think you will need some cash for a house, car, vacation or other major commitment over the next six to twenty-four months, then it is advisable to keep that specific amount of money in a cash money market fund. It is certainly wise to keep an emergency fund amount in money market funds in order to handle the curveballs that life throws at you. Otherwise, use cash mainly as a reserve to give you flexibility within your master stock portfolio. Cash is not at all like John Elway, and it will never rally to win the championship for you.

* * *

Like slack tide, the ebb and flow of a boxing match can go nowhere. Ali versus Foreman. Lewis versus Tyson. Then out of nowhere, one of the fighters starts to take charge, first with a flurry of punches to the midsection that weakens the opponent's knees. Then comes a hard left hook to the jaw, and the next thing you know the opponent is on the mat, blood spurting from the corner of his mouth.

The referee goes to a three count, then four, five, and six. The losing fighter gets to one knee, then after what seems like a two-minute commercial, gets to his feet and clumsily tries to regain control over his body.

The fight may go on for a while, but the downed fighter has no positive momentum. In fact, at this point he probably has negative momentum. He may have looked good on paper, he may have even been the Las Vegas favorite, but in his present state, it will be difficult, if not impossible, for him to make a comeback.

The same thing can happen to a favorite, heavyweight stock under the bright lights of Wall Street. If a stock goes down hard on the mat, it may be able to rally and get back up on one knee, but it may be a very long time before the stock heals enough to regain any truly positive long-term momentum.

Like the boxer, the stock price is battered. In this situation, investor psychology surrounding the stock is usually bruised and broken. Why? The reason is not the important thing, and does not matter. Take your signal from the events in the ring. They show that confidence in the stock has been overpowered by doubt and uncertainty. The rehab process may take place, but it may take a long time. In the foreseeable future, the broken stock will most likely lack power, like that broken and battered boxer.

Don't even worry about analyzing why the fight went wrong. Act by moving on to a better contender.

* * *

If you were in the market for a racehorse, would you rather buy one thoroughbred colt with strong bloodlines, or an entire herd of wild mustangs with questionable heritage? Most of us would rather invest in one "quality" animal and when given the choice, attempt to buy the best of the breed. If you were in the market for a used car, would you prefer to buy one certified pre-owned vehicle, or a six-pack of old fixer-uppers? Hopefully you would prefer to buy the certified vehicle, even though it might cost more, because you have sound business judgment. The certified vehicle would be more reliable while you owned it, and it would have greater market value if you wanted to resell it.

Common sense says that we should buy stock assests the same way, much like a business buys an item for its inventory. We should buy quality, enjoy some present benefit from it, and then have the flexibility to sell it and transfer that value to some other investor at some future date.

Why not consider approaching the company stocks that you invest in from the same perspective? Although there are no guarantees in the world of business, quality often prevails over meaningful periods of time. It is hard to go wrong if you always consider the best bloodlines, and the best of the breed. In the stock market, quality is often found in great companies that are dominant in their chosen field of business; names like Disney, Coke, and Wal-Mart.

That said, many RSIs (rookie stock investors) are attracted to stocks that represent anything but quality, and often trade for less than $5 a share. These investors have the misconception that if the stock price is really low, then the potential for profits must be really high. They just don't get it. Sure, it is possible that a decision to buy a low priced stock may work out favorably, but the odds of that happening are slim at best.

Consider the following tale of two high profile companies, Target vs. K-Mart. Target Corporation stock (Target Stores, Marshall Fields) was the higher priced choice in 1999, trading around $28 per share, but many serious investors owned it and considered it to be a quality growth company with great bloodlines. Over the next three years the price of Target common stock grew by more than 40%, to $40 per share by early 2002. Not bad. All along the way the investment represented quality, and top-tier financial strength.

By comparison, in 1999, at almost the same time that Target Corporation traded at $28, K-Mart common stock traded at around $4 per share. Low price? Yes. Bargain? Maybe, maybe not. Over the same time frame we described above, K-Mart stock deteriorated to a price of $1, and the company actually declared Chapter 11 bankruptcy in early 2002.

At the time of this writing, no one can say where K-Mart is going, while Target is still going strong. This is just one pitch in a bullpen full of examples, and past performance is not a guarantee of future performance. However, this is an example to file away in your memory bank and call up the next time you have the urge to buy a "happy meal" (TM: McDonald's Corp.) stock for less than $5.

* * *

Every baseball fan has witnessed a great pickoff move, by a leftie like Tom Glavine, that places an unsuspecting base-runner in a rundown between first and second base. No place to go. No-man's land. The chances of something good happening to bail out the frozen base-runner in a situation like this are slim at best.

A stock price can get caught in a similar, difficult situation, where it is literally too late to sell and too early to buy more. In the market of 2000, an example was Cisco systems, a high-profile stock that broke down through key support levels at $60, and then $50, and then cascaded all the way down to the $20 area.

When any stock goes through that kind of train wreck, investor sentiment towards it becomes mixed and murky. Complacent shareholders who did not protect their portfolios with sell-stop orders feel frustrated and beaten. Their egos will not allow them to sell a stock at $20 that was previously at $60, because that would make them look foolish.

At the same time, many potential buyers view a stock like our Cicso example as damaged goods, because the sentiment and the technical trend indicators are negative. The stock has been in reverse, so it will have to shift into neutral before it will have any chance of shifting into first gear. Time must pass for a rehab and repair process to take place.

It is generally not prudent to rush in and bottom feed by buying any stock that has recently been marked down by 50% or more. Sure, the stock may bounce a little, but unless some major fundamental event occurs, it may need to wander around in no-man's land for a while. That's because major trends tend to remain in place until time and events break them, and ultimately reverse them.

Picture a pro quarterback who gets nailed by a 6′ 6,″ 290-pound defensive end. The medical report shows that the q.b. has bruised ribs and a broken wrist, and he is out of commission for four to six weeks. He's in no-man's land, and he is not going anyplace until a period of recovery and rehabilitation takes place.

Muddy water let stand, will clear.

Confucius

Similarly, time for repair and rehabilitation is often critical in the case of a wounded stock. A major trend will re-emerge, but it may take a lot of time to establish itself. The waters will clear, and a broken stock may gradually regain its strength, but then again, it may not. In the meantime, the market will present better opportunities for your portfolio. Just as a savvy baseball fan knows that a runner caught in a rundown between first and second is a guy in trouble, a savvy investor knows that a stock in no-man's land is a stock in trouble.

* * *

At the racetrack, long shots come in once in a while. In the National League, pitchers hit home runs once in a while. In the NFL, quarterbacks make tackles after interceptions once in a while. But over long periods of time and many trials, the reality is that each of these events is rare. The dark horse at the track, the pitcher at the plate, and the quarterback after an interception are all relatively poor bets to succeed.

Similarly, companies that have fragile business models are poor investment risks. In a perfect world, the management at companies considering going public should have developed a business model that has a high probability of being profitable within a reasonable period of time. In the late 1990s, startup Internet companies raised huge amounts of cash through initial public offerings. The problem was that some of them had fragile business models based upon variables such as cash flow and capture ratios, rather than real, measurable corporate earnings. In hindsight, the percentage of these startups that were unsuccessful is staggering. The post-mortem is that the frenzy of the late nineties sucked thousands of unsuspecting investors into these stocks like the undertow of the ocean.

Admittedly, over shorter windows of time, the trend of a company's stock market value can certainly be out of sync with the trend of a company's earnings. As an example, stocks of established automobile companies sometimes begin up-trends during periods when company profits and earnings still are absolutely miserable.

Regardless, over longer periods that include various business climates, a company that you are considering for investment should have a history of stable and increasing earnings per share. It does not have to be a perfect formula, but a generally positive pattern should be recognizable, indicating that senior management has a vision and a business model founded upon consistency and profitability. Novice Internet investors of the last decade learned the hard way that smoke and mirrors have little long-term value when you are building a common stock portfolio.

CHAPTER FOURTEEN:

THE SECOND TIME AROUND

It happened in the case of Raphael Palmeiro. His career included a early stint with the Texas Rangers that ended after the 1993 season. After he moved on to play five years for the Baltimore Orioles from 1994 through 1998, the Texas rangers were willing to sign him a second time at a much higher price (contract value). Let the record show that his 1993 salary with the Rangers was $4.6 million, and the annual salary he re-signed for in 1999 was $8.8 million.

Isn't it interesting that multi-million dollar sports franchises are sometimes willing to risk millions of dollars to re-sign a quality player at a higher price? Circumstances change and times change, so they are willing to pay more for the investment in a quality player. The value of any asset, be it a ballplayer, a business, or a building, changes over time.

The year was . . .?

Redskins defeat Dolphins in Super Bowl
Motorola begins testing cellular phone service in Chicago
Islanders defeat Oilers for Stanley Cup
The final episode of Mash airs to a record TV audience
Baltimore wins World Series over Philadelphia
Dow Jones Industrial Average closes the year at 1,259

The year was . . . 1983.

Yet, amazingly, some investors refuse to buy the same stock they once owned at a higher price the second time around because they view that act as a sign of failure. These investors lock themselves out of accumulating great stocks that might fit their current objectives, just because they once owned it at a lower price. Their myopia, probably brought on by regret over selling in the first place, leads them to the misconception that to buy the stock at a second, higher price is the ultimate confirmation of failure.

The real failure is that these investors do not realize that the past should never rule the present. If the fundamental and technical elements that drive a stock's value have changed for the better, then the purchase at a new, higher price could actually turn out to be a great business decision. If the signals are positive, do it. After all, it's strictly business. There is nothing personal about it, and the act of buying a company at a higher price has nothing to do with your ultimate potential for success or failure as a serious investor.

Keep the same perspective as the senior management of a sports team that re-signs a franchise player. Based upon what you know about this marketplace and this asset right now, is this business decision a good one? That's the only question that matters.

One of the toughest things for the rookie investor to do is to buy a stock that is trading at a new fifty-two week high. In this age of Best Buy and Costco, it goes against our nature to buy anything at a price higher than the last guy.

In order to get over this issue, you may need to do what successful VSIs do. Don't limit your thoughts or your actions because of past barriers. Don't ever be afraid to buy a stock that is trading at a new high if the signals supporting that strength are readable. Recognize the economic fact that if a stock is at a new high, every investor who owns that stock has a profit, and must be relatively happy with it. That alone can be a great stabilizing factor in the land of stock investing, because all of the unhappy investors who wanted to "get out when they got back to even" have probably sold out of the stock on the way up. That may mean that demand is overtaking supply, which could lead to an even higher value if that uptrend continues.

A stock is never too high to buy or too low to sell.

Jesse Livermore
Legendary Investor, Early 1900s

A problem is that it is the nature of novice investors to view a stock's fifty-two week trading range as normal, when in the market there is no such thing as normal. If a stock has traded between $30 and $40 over the past twelve months, RSIs often think that it will continue to trade between $30 and $40. They become frozen in the comfort of the past trading range, which may no longer be a reasonable benchmark in the moving target known as the market.

Psychologists call this thought process "anchoring," which can become a problem when the crowd places too much significance on past trading ranges, such as twelve-month highs and lows. At the beginning of the 2001 season, many sports writers probably thought that Brett Boone would hit around eighteen to twenty home runs that season. Why? At that time his average over his eight-year major league playing career was seventeen long balls per year, so eighteen to twenty sounded reasonable because it was in his historic hitting range. The end of the story is that Bret Boone hit thirty-seven home runs in the 2001 season, 210% above his "historical average" of seventeen. That's a breakout. The reasons for the breakout are not important. The important fact is that past trading ranges and performance ranges are overrated. Circumstances change, the landscape changes, supply and demand relationships change. Don't get caught placing too much emphasis on past trading ranges, because they may not be as meaningful as many of the other great variables that are available to you as a savvy investor.

Over the past ten years, it's a given that a countless number of individual investors refused to buy some of the great American growth companies because they were trading at new price highs at that particular moment. Consider the following examples, adjusted for stock splits: In 1996, Home Depot common stock was trading at a "new high" of $13. By 1999, it traded above $40 per share. In 1995, Microsoft was trading at a "new high" of $13. By 1999, it traded north of $100 per share.

In each of these cases, $13 was actually a very lucky number, and any investor who hesitated to buy these stocks at these 52-week price highs missed out on huge opportunities. No one can forecast when this type of thing will play out in the future, but let these examples confirm that a stock trading at a twelve-month high can turn out to be a very good deal. If the proper positive signals are present, don't be afraid to start to accumulate a stock that is at a new high. After all, if you buy high, you just might be able to sell higher.

The various stock exchanges allow buy and sell orders to be placed in several different ways. A "limit" order gives the instruction that you are willing to make a transaction at a specific price level. It is a signal that you want to take an action, either to buy or to sell, at a specific price and nothing more in the case of a buy order, or at a specific price and nothing less in the case of a sell order.

On the other hand, a "market" order sends the instruction to the stock exchange that you are willing to buy or sell a specific stock at the current, prevailing price level. Note that most of our study has focused on highly capitalized, established, domestic companies. In a fast-paced auction marketplace where millions of shares change hands on a daily basis, a "market" order gives you a high probability of making your desired transaction within a range of a few pennies per share from the last reported price. State-of-the-art satellite communications systems give you the ability to execute a market order from any place in the country within a matter of seconds. Although possible, it is rare that the cadence of a company's stock price would change markedly over a period of less than a minute, since any current market price represents a certain equilibrium between buyers and sellers.

What if the guy who worked across the street was attempting to buy a block of "American Running Shoe" stock at precisely the same time as you. His instructions are to buy at market, while yours are to buy at a price limited, or defined, by a specific reported price. He is Mr. Market Order, and you are Mr. Limit Order. What would happen if "American Running Shoe" stock moved up five cents per share just before these two distinct orders hit the system. Mr. Market Order owns the stock. Done. Mission accomplished. You, Mr. Limit Order, do not yet own the stock. For now, you have missed it. Your stress level immediately increases. What you thought was going to be one decision has now turned into at least two decisions. Should you change your original limit price instruction? Should you wait and pray?

Now, suppose you are in Mr. Murphy's world, and the situation worsens. Suppose the market for "American Running Shoe" stock continues to move away from you, like a mountain range in the rearview mirror. You have a problem, because you still do not own the stock.

This writer, along with most veteran stock investors, has experienced the same type of highly frustrating situation. I have seen a stock that I missed because of a limit price on a buy order move up twenty points from my brilliantly placed limit order. By trying to get fancy and save a few pennies per share, I have totally missed opportunities to own stocks that have gone up and never looked back.

Similar experiences can happen when you are attempting to sell, but because negative moves in the market are even more violent than positive moves, a stock can move away from you at an even faster pace. When the sentiment regarding a stock turns negative, the selling pressure can take on the characteristics of a frenzied crowd trying to get out of a crowded movie theater. The pressure may cause a freefall that results in a fast-moving market that is hard to keep up with, especially if you use limit orders.

Missing a market because of a limit order is an error made by almost every VSI who would admit it. You try to finesse a solid business decision by gaining a little more control over the execution price, you miss the stock, it moves away from you, and you're left watching it from the cheap seats. Trust me when I say that if this happens to you just once, you will probably remember the experience for a very long time.

A limit order that does not get executed is as bad as the play that you should have run with two minutes remaining in your last game. It is as bad as that sinking feeling about the pitch that you should have thrown in the top of the ninth inning in your last game. How can you avoid the gut-wrenching frustration of the "limit" order that did not get filled? Simple. First, strive to buy, sell, and own stock in large companies that trade actively and efficiently on the New York Stock Exchange, the American Stock Exchange, or the NASDAQ. Secondly, use "market" orders without fail. Do this, not part of the time, but all the time. When you decide to make a buy or sell transaction, check the prevailing price level, and then make the trade at the market. If you want to make the trip, get on the team bus. Pull the trigger. Make the transaction. Do this, and you will never find yourself worrying about nickels and dimes in the land of $100 bills.

It is not the same to talk of bulls, as to enter the bullring.

Spanish Proverb

Interesting investment theories, you say, but "I think I'll just track them and test them with a Monopoly money portfolio for a while," much like a college student in a finance class. While you certainly have the right to take that approach, I cannot agree with it.

Why? Consider this. Could a totally untested rookie golfer read five how-to books on golf in the comfort of his own family room and then go out and break ninety, or even 100? Probably not, because one of the secrets to success in the activities that we know as "sports" is to practice in game-like situations. As a serious investor, you will improve much faster if you take the same action-oriented approach.

In 1973 and 1974, during one of the fiercest bear markets of the past century, I was in business school. Sure, we studied the day-to-day damage in the stock market, as we considered various investment theories and methodologies, but even that experience was nothing like being on the playing field in a real-time game situation. That type of experience and those battle scars would come later, when I experienced the turbulent markets of 1981, 1987, 1990, and 2001.

One must learn by doing the thing, for though you think you know it, you have no certainty until you try.

Aristotle
Greek Philosopher

Training camp drills without pads have their place, but nothing can compare to the rush of the real deal, and to practice at full speed in full gear. Sooner or later, if you want to experience the joy of winning, you must be motivated to make real money in real-time markets. You don't have to go up against a 300-pound lineman in the first session, but you must increase the cash that you invest, and the responsibility that you take for your own results.

He who stops being better, stops being good.

Oliver Cromwell,
Author

Even overtime hockey games eventually come to an end. The longest nine-inning baseball game on record, played between the Los Angeles Dodgers and the San Francisco Giants on October 5, 2001, finally came to an end (final score Dodgers 11-Giants 10) (Time: 4 hours, 27 minutes).

Although even the best and the worst sports seasons come to an end, in the market it doesn't work that way. The market just keeps on ticking with the drum-like cadence of a New York City Marathon. You, as a serious investor with long-term objectives, must pace yourself. The markets don't stop, but that doesn't mean that you have to be 100% in the market all the time.

Players in all the major professional sports have down time. They go to Hawaii, or they go fishing in Idaho, or, if they are fortunate enough to win the Super Bowl, maybe they even go to Disney Land. Like the rhythm of the heartbeat, there is pressure, then a period of rest. There is wear and tear, then a period for repair.

The markets won't give you that luxury, so you will have to make it for yourself. There are times when you should be less than fully invested in the markets, and there are times when you should be out of the market altogether. Although muscles can take a lot of stress, after a tear the body needs a period for repair. Since the market will never just hand you an off-season pass, you must learn to create your own off-season periods of reflection, rest, and repair.

After all, they don't call it the "Daytona 50," they call it the "Daytona 500." No one really cares who is ahead at the fifty-mile checkpoint. As you participate in the great race known as an investing career, pace yourself, and you will be able to stay in the race longer than you ever imagined.

He who does not risk, never gets to drink champagne.

Russian proverb

When psychologists ask elderly people the question about "regret," what do you think the most common response is? The question, to be specific, goes like this. "When you think about your life's experiences, do you have more regret over the things you did, or the things you did not attempt to do?" Overwhelmingly, researchers find that we, as human beings, hold the most regret over the things that we did not attempt to do.

Free markets, exemplified by the U.S. system of investing, are a fundamental part of our economic and social system, and we all should be ever thankful for that. There is no commandment that states that you must ever invest in the stock market. After all, the choice is yours. There is no commandment that states that you must seek to enhance your quality of life, either, but you are taking the time to read a book like this because you evidently believe in exploring new possibilities and new strategies. Good for you.

> *Far better it is to dare mighty things, to win glorious triumphs even though checkered by failures, than rank with those poor spirits who neither enjoy much nor suffer much because they live in the gray twilight that knows neither victory or defeat.*
>
> ***Theodore Roosevelt***
> ***American President***

Some say we should not believe everything we hear. Maybe the saying should be, don't believe everything you *fear*, because uncontrolled fear can be a debilitating thing. We'll look at that more in the next section. For now, avoid the knockout punch while maintaining the knockout upside potential of the market. Load up, and fire all your bullets. Seek out new challenges, sound decisions, and wealth accumulation without regret. Seek to enhance your quality of life, enjoy the journey, and drink champagne.

The Offense: Checklist

1. Diversify, but concentrate. Twenty to twenty-five positions is a reasonable number for a diversified stock portfolio.
2. Diversify by sector. This process can be compared to diversifying the players on a sports team by talent and specific skill set.
3. Use an "elevator system" to scale into positions.
4. Use a "harvest system" to scale out of positions.
5. Seek out the "sweet spot" by using "dual analysis," a system based on both fundamental analysis and technical analysis. The strength of "fundamental" is determining what to buy. The strength of "technical" is determining when to buy it, and when to sell it.

6. One of the key indicators in the battle between supply and demand in the marketplace is the relationship between the current price and the 200-day moving average. Always be aware of the green light (attack), yellow light (balance), red light (control) signal of the overall market, as well as for every individual stock that you own or are considering for purchase.
7. Use "boundary limits" (chalk-lines) to control any single position in your portfolio to 6% or less.
8. Always remain confident in the historical upward bias of the U.S. markets and the free market system.
9. If the proper signal is there, do not hesitate to buy a stock at a new price high. To buy high and sell higher is a viable strategy in a bull market.
10. U.S. Treasury bills (and money market funds) do not rally. "He who does not risk never drinks champagne."

SECTION FOUR:
THE SPECIAL TEAMS (A MEETING WITH THE SPECIAL TEAMS COACH)

CHAPTER FIFTEEN:

SPECIAL TEAMS AND SPECIAL APPROACHES

If you still question the fact that great coaches and great business leaders often think alike, consider the following quotes and their sources. As you read the following, imagine the same things being said by your favorite head coach.

> *We view today . . . as our very best day. We are built to play offense and to play it now.*
>
> ***Jeffrey R. Immelt***
> ***Chairman and C.E.O.***
> ***General Electric Annual Report 2001***

> *If fielding the right team gets us in the game, motivating our players is the way to win.*
>
> ***Kenneth D. Lewis***
> ***Chairman and C.E.O.***
> ***Bank of America Corp. Annual Report 2001***

> *This game will be won or lost based upon the intensity of our efforts . . .*
>
> ***William T. Esrey***
> ***Chairman and C.E.O.***
> ***Sprint Annual Report 2001***

During the past year the . . . team has developed a clear direction . . . and demonstrated early momentum on the implementation of the . . . plan.

What I discovered was an extremely intelligent team with the absolute desire to win . . . The key to any strategy lies in the strength of its execution.

Terry S. Semel
Chairman and C.E.O.
Yahoo! 2001 Annual Report

We know that our ultimate success depends on the quality of our . . . execution.

Andrew S. Grove
Chairman
Intel Corp. 2001 Annual Report

Together we have the opportunity to build on the momentum of this past year's accomplishments and create a strong future. (We) are committed to our tradition of winning . . .

Allen Questrom
Chairman and C.E.O.
J.C. Penney Co., Inc. 2001 Annual Report

These contemporary comments came from leaders of some of the great companies in America. Any one of these statements could have been made in a boardroom, or in a locker room. See the similarities. Who said that it's not all the same game?

* * *

In the 1978 NFL season, he threw twenty interceptions, or an average of more than one interception per game (Not a great stat). More importantly, that year he led the AFC in passing with twenty-eight touchdowns and 2,915 passing yards, and he was the top passer in the league. He remains the only quarterback in history to lead his team to four Super Bowl victories. A key reason Terry Bradshaw became an exceptional Steeler quarterback is because he was great at overcoming errors. In that 1978 season, he suffered through twenty interceptions, plus 141 incomplete passes, plus numerous sacks and busted plays. That adds up to a lot of errors. Bradshaw survived them all, brought home the AFC passing title, and helped the Steelers win Super Bowl XXIII.

Steve Young is the highest rated passer in NFL history, but the record shows that he threw 1,482 passes that were "incomplete" over his fifteen-year career.

Dan Marino threw for more yardage and more touchdowns than any NFL quarterback in history. He threw for over 61,000 yards and 420 touchdowns, but he also threw 3,391 "incomplete" passes.

Success is simply moving from failure to failure without loss of enthusiasm.

Winston Churchill
British Statesman

Moving from failure to failure was just a part of the winning formula for Bradshaw and this bunch, just as it is for most of the regular guys who grow to become legends. With the great ones, it's not about the errors, it's about the way they manipulate errors into success. Errors? Yes. Losers? I don't think so. To the great athlete, success really is nothing more than the manipulation of errors. In the words of Churchill, it is moving from failure to failure with an almost childlike, unwavering level of enthusiasm.

The year was . . .?

Bears defeat Patriots in Super Bowl
Microsoft Corp. goes public
Mets over Red Sox in World Series
Penn State is ranked #1 in final NCAA football poll
News Corp. launches the Fox television network
The Dow Jones Industrial Average closes the year at . . . 1896

The year was . . . 1986.

In the end, the difference between great athletes and mediocre athletes is not the number of errors they make, it's the way they deal with the errors they make. The great ones manipulate errors into something less negative, almost to the point where they mentally "minimize" their errors like a computer document, put them in the "recycle bin," or even delete them totally from the important data retained on their mental hard drive.

We know that a plane flying from Chicago to Los Angeles is actually "off course" more than 90% of the time. It may be only a few degrees off course, but it is still off course. Skilled pilots, modern instrumentation, and autopilot technology make it possible for a plane to proceed on a smooth course rather than some jagged plot that takes it over Salt Lake and Santa Fe. To a professional pilot, being off course, and taking the requisite action to compensate is just a part of the process of air travel. To Terry Bradshaw, throwing an interception once in a while was just a part of the process. To a successful investor, being slightly off course is just a part of the process. After all, in the end, the most important thing about a flight, a season, or an investing career is not the exact course, but the successful completion of the journey.

You can have incredible success (financial or otherwise) by being less than perfect. Ask Terry Bradshaw. Four Super Bowl rings. NFL Hall of Fame, Class of 1989.

* * *

He was nicknamed for the Missouri town of his birth. He was a rebellious kid, but he found baseball, and it became the prescription that balanced his youth. Although he never had great physical talent, he had a great mind for the game, and over time he grew to become a true baseball man.

The end of the story is that his baseball career spanned forty-three years, and he was elected to the Major League Baseball Hall of Fame in 1966. Over one twelve-year span in his legendary career (1949-1960) he managed the Yankees to ten pennants and seven World Series titles. Yet buried in the box scores of his life story is the fact that Casey Stengel lost 49% . . . yes, 49% . . . of all the games that he managed at the big league level. (The record shows that he coached in 1,905 victories and 1,842 defeats over his forty-three-year career.

Was Casey Stengel a loser? Most experts would say "no way." He holds a positive place in the folklore of twentieth century baseball, and was an innovator when it came to platooning players and situation baseball. He managed Mantle and Ford and Berra on those dominant Yankee teams of the 1950's, but he may actually be remembered as much for coming out of retirement to manage a new franchise known as the New York Mets (1962 through 1965, when he was in his seventies).

What if Stengel had taken losing personally, and quit it all after his 100th loss? Or his 200th loss? There is no way that he would have attained such a high place in baseball history. Casey was "old school," a guy who never got overly emotional regarding one game, win or lose. Think about his career losses (1,842), and look inside the numbers for a minute. Considering that there are 162 games in a season, (prior to 1961, there were only 154 games in a season) that means that he experienced the equivalent of more than "eleven" complete big league seasons with nothing but losses.

As you think back about the things you are good at in life, like golf, public speaking, or working with computer programs, I challenge you to come up with anything meaningful that was totally easy the first time out. If you say that riding a bicycle, or public speaking, or hitting a fastball, or setting up a spreadsheet was a piece of cake the first time you tried it, you're probably lying (or you have a poor memory). That's the way it's meant to be. Virtually every activity in life that matters to us was difficult before it became easy. So, even at this stage of reading investment books like this one, don't worry about it if you're still having trouble accepting these ideas. Accept the fact that these strategies will become easier with practice, just like the other great things that you enjoy in life.

In the sporting games, and the investing games, sometimes you must give up control to gain control. A big problem is that many of us have grown up in a society that emphasizes "control" as a very important key to success. In the sporting world we hear references made about "control" all the time, as in "control the clock," or "control the ball," or "control your breaking pitch." As hard as it may be to do, it is time to relax your attitude about control, because you simply have no command over many of the external variables that affect the investment process.

You will be better off if you take on the more relaxed attitude shared by most all-star players and all-star investors. Think about the simple statement "see the ball, read the ball, hit the ball." The great hitters who repeat and practice that mantra have come to the realization that "I can't control the speed of the pitch, or the break of the pitch, but I can control how I react to it." They share the attitude of the relaxed investor who believes, "I can't control the market, but I have the ability to read and interpret the signals that the market gives me."

"See the market, read the market, react to the market." Successful investors who have achieved a level of balance in their personal and business lives have come to the realization that, "I can't control the trend of the market, or the trend of my specific stocks, but I can control how I react to those trends."

No matter what decisions you make, or what reactions you make, they are not the ultimate measure of your chances of succeeding as an investor. Because of your prudent approach to position boundaries and risk control, no single investment decision will lead to your ultimate success or failure as an investor. Any investment decision you make today is just one of the next 100 investment decisions that you are going to make. Mentally condition yourself like the hitter who says to himself, "this at-bat is just one of my next 100 at-bats."

Sure, we must prepare and do our homework, but there comes a time when we must pull the trigger and make a sound business decision based upon the information that we have available to us at that moment. Any decision of a great head coach is the sum total of all of his mental readings regarding that game and that game situation. Even if three of his best players are injured, he must work with the healthy players he has on the roster that particular day.

Consider this hypothetical football situation. Imagine that you are Steve Spurrier, the head coach of the Redskins, in a game against your division rivals, the Dallas Cowboys. It's the final game of the regular season, and you need a win to make the playoffs. You have a strong pass offense, and you have confidence in your guys to run a specific play-action pass. You call that play midway through the first period, and it fails miserably. In fact, it results in an interception that is returned for thirty yards. Would you, as the head coach, feel the sting of failure in your gut for a few seconds? If you're human, of course you would.

Now consider a tougher question. Would you call the same play in the fourth quarter of the same game with the game on the line? You bet you would. The stated facts of the situation are that you have confidence in your offensive players, and you have confidence in your offensive game plan. Yes, the play failed once, but you would call the same play in the same game if the situation warranted it, not just because you are gutsy, but because you have an unshaken level of confidence in your players and in your plan.

To a rational head coach, the idea of taking one play, or even one game, personally simply doesn't compute. When it comes to your investment "play-calling," follow the lead of great contemporary coaches like Mike Shanahan, Phil Jackson, and Joe Torre. Sometimes they exhibit great calmness, and sometimes they exhibit great emotion, but they have so much confidence in their respective systems that they simply will not let one incident compromise them.

As you mature into the fraternity of great investors, train yourself in the ways of the fearless head coach. With a morning blend of confidence, discipline, and mental conditioning, you can overcome any urge to take things personally, if you are anchored by the belief that the outcome of your outside investment decisions has nothing to do with your inner self-worth.

In the world of business decisions, stress is a pollutant that surrounds us most of the time, whether we like it or not. With that in mind, consider the following chain of events. Say that you study a specific stock and make a business decision to buy it, and buy an initial position for $100 a share on Monday at 10 a.m. By noon on Tuesday, for reasons that were beyond your control, the stock has fallen 5% to $95. Being human, your stress level increases a notch. By 2 p.m. on that same Tuesday, the stock is down almost 8%, and your stress level needle edges across the dial. Ten minutes later your protective sell stop order is triggered and you are out of the stock at $90.80, for a 9.2% loss, and all of this happened in less than thirty-six hours.

Is this situation stressful for you? Of course it is. After all, you were forced to take a 9% loss on your original investment before the check had arrived in the mail.

What are the sources of stress? It's pretty simple. An event that you had no control over derailed your best-laid plans. A good idea turned into a bad event. A new stock investment that triggers a sell-stop in the first two days is kind of like a pitcher who gives up a three-run homer in the top of the first inning. A positive game plan played out in the form of a negative event. It's normal for you to feel some stress.

Since you are a logical guy, you know that you should attempt to neutralize the stress of the situation. That's where your "objectivity" comes in to play, because any level of "objectivity" that you can mentally force into the equation surrounding a negative event should lessen and neutralize the stress of that event. It's analogous to a view from the other sideline, or the other dugout, and it can offer a fresh change of perspective when it may be needed most. Like a workout after a tough day, a shot of objectivity can work to neutralize your negative perception of an event, and the stress that it has caused you.

The perception of the other fans in the stadium of life should have little influence on you. In fact, the more "meaningless" the majority view is to you, the better. Since your perception of events is the crucial component, as you neutralize your feelings about any negative event with a strong dose of objectivity, you will be on your way to a richer life, and you might even make some money along the way. With less stress, your activities in the market will play out more like soft jazz than hard rock, and your objectivity will continue to reward you in ways that you never imagined.

CHAPTER SIXTEEN:

YOUR PORTFOLIO IS NOT ONE BIG EMERGENCY

The various financial news networks would love for you to think of your portfolio as one big emergency. They even use action verbs to describe the capital markets in ways commonly reserved for human beings. Today the market "tumbled, or soared, or slipped, or plummeted, or raced." By attempting to give life to some inanimate financial object, the cable networks seek to hook our attention so that we will spend more of each day glued to their network watching their talking-head guests. After all, the goal of the public media is to maintain and increase viewers. If more of us become a part of the herd, the network's ratings rise, and that leads to increased advertising revenues, and so on, and so on, and so on.

When we allow ourselves to be hypnotized into watching these networks during every market minute, we play right into the hype of "stock tickers" and minute-by-minute pricing. Sadly, I know investors who have watched the minute-by-minute ticker for years in order to check on the prices of the same stocks that they have owned "for years." Think about that. It makes about as much sense as measuring a cross-country road trip with a yardstick.

In retrospect, a case can be made that the traders who had the most trouble with the capital markets during the "dot-com" frenzy of the late nineties were the ones who never learned to separate themselves from the noise of the financial networks. All too often they set themselves up for failure when the momentum markets faltered and minute-by-minute monitoring became less attractive.

Granted, tickers with instant stock quotes serve a purpose. They accommodate investors who must sell at that minute because of specific personal circumstances. Maybe those investors must generate cash to settle an estate, or pay taxes, or pay for some emergency. For the rest of us, real-time quotes should be viewed as an appraisal, nothing more and nothing less. For some strange reason, many members of the instant breakfast generation find comfort in instant appraisals of stocks that they have no intention of selling. As a serious, but savvy investor, if you do not have a desire to sell right now, a more healthy approach may be to review your portfolio daily, or even weekly. After all, if you follow the risk control strategies that we have reviewed, you are insured against catastrophic loss through the use of sell-stop orders. A daily portfolio review, away from the noise and the activity of market hours, makes a lot of sense. Isn't it true that even the President often deals with daily briefings regarding various world events? With the proper protective coverage, daily detailed reviews of your portfolio and your watch list will be much more meaningful to you than the emotional drain of hours spent watching minute-by-minute stock quotes dance across a TV screen.

The year was . . .?

Dallas defeats Pittsburgh in Super Bowl
Tiger Woods is Sports Illustrated Sportsman of the Year
Yahoo goes public
Bulls over Sonics for NBA title
Yankees defeat Braves in World Series
Dow Jones Industrial Average closes the year at . . .6,448

The year was . . . 1996.

This is not to say that you should construct a stock portfolio, put it in a desk drawer, and forget about it. Monitor from a distance, like a wise scout who sits high up in the stands. Use the protective sell-stop order disciplines and position limits that we have reviewed here so that you are always insured against catastrophic loss. Don't let one event, or one punch, flatten you. Get on with the other important things in your life. Spend more time with your family and loved ones. Do something creative. Work on improving your career. Work on improving your body and your mind. The fact that one of your stocks is up half a point, or down a point, is an uncontrollable inhuman aspect of your day that should have little or no impact on the more meaningful, human aspects of your day.

> *Life is what happens to us while we're busy planning something else.*
>
> ***John Lennon***
> ***The Beatles***

If you take out the proper insurance on your stocks, then why not consider checking the value of your portfolio only once a day, or even once every few days. On a road trip, it's not logical to focus on the highway ten feet in front of your car. As a sensible driver, you focus on a bigger, broader, peripheral picture of the road and the surroundings several hundred yards in front of you. Do the same thing with your portfolio. Don't let the financial networks control your life (if the financial networks control your life, do you really have a life?) If you plant a pecan tree, do you dig it up every day to see how the root system is doing? No. Then why not back off a little bit?

I make these statements with confidence because history proves that time has been the ally of U.S. investors for the past 200 years. Time will continue to be your ally, if you will just let it. Historically, the market has an upward bias, shown by the fact that the market average for large established U.S. companies has grown at an average annual rate in excess of 10% over the past eighty years. History has blessed U.S. stock investors with a long-term positive trend, interrupted by temporary periods of significant negative corrections. A sharp, but nevertheless, serious correction in the market that clears out the excesses is like a fire caused by lightning that clears out some of the excess growth in a national forest. These are both natural events, and nothing to fear.

Corrections are a natural part of the process, like a leopard that culls the weak from the herd. Back away from the minute-by-minute details, and develop confidence in the market system, and in your own M.O.S. (market operating system). Sometimes you gain a better perspective from a distance than from a front row seat anyway. A defensive linesman in the middle of the playing field has a much more limited perspective on the play than the defensive coordinator in the coaches booth fifty yards away.

Even Stephen Spielberg, one of the creative geniuses of our time, has said that he sometimes views the footage of his current film project without audio, in order to get a clearer perspective on the flow and the message of the motion picture. That may be the greatest endorsement of all for turning off the sound of the cable TV networks. Avoid the noise of the financial news networks, and give time a chance to become your ally. Contrary to what the financial news networks would like you to believe, your portfolio is not one big emergency.

* * *

How do they do it? Referees, officials, and umpires, that is. They do the job that is required of them at that moment in time, and then they move on. They see it, they call it, and then they get on with their work.

A good referee doesn't get in the way of the action, does he? In fact, the true test may be that if a game was well officiated, most fans would not even remember much about the officials who called the game. It's a tough assignment, but as a true professional, a good umpire must face each situation without hesitation, and without the benefit of instant replay. Any game of sport is predictably unpredictable, so we are blessed as sports fans when the officiating or umpiring is highly predictable.

To be a good cornerback, you need a bad memory.

John Madden

Former Coach, TV Analyst

Even though Madden was talking about defensive backs at the time of this quote, he would probably say the same thing about officials and referees. The best officials approach their craft with a bad memory. Their job is too important to dwell on past calls or past judgments. After all, one call, or one missed call, isn't that important in determining how he ranks among his peers over a long career.

As a successful investor, regardless of whether you make a decision that generates a loss or a profit, it is wise to file the decision away, so that it will not have an impact on your next decision. Move on, and stand ready to call the same play again if a similar situation sets up in front of you.

We all know that there are times when your success may require an action that is instinctively uncomfortable. The hometown fans may be restless, or they may want to remember a call from the previous game, but the true professional knows that he must forget it. Otherwise, that bias and fear of making bad calls can haunt him, and actually lead to more bad calls. A weak approach and poor judgment can spiral down into more and more negatives. Never let one bad call get the best of you. File it away and move on, because there's more action in front of you. Remember, there's a lot more time left in the game.

We have said that in order to become more realistic about your personal investment objectives, it may be helpful to review the process in slow motion, like a frame-by-frame review of a game film. Another way to say this is:

Think slowly; act quickly.

Greek Proverb

Sometimes to think slowly leads to thinking outside the box. Popularized by information technology companies over the past decade, the phrase "thinking outside the box" is a great metaphor for the idea of attacking a problem from a fresh, innovative perpective. Situations sometimes take on a whole new meaning when we stand apart from the crowd, and make a concerted effort to view things as a contrarian.

For instance, take a shot at this situation. A dime is in an old wine bottle. The bottle is corked. How do you get the dime out of the bottle without breaking the bottle. The solution may not be readily apparent to you, unless you expand mentally and think outside the box. A logical solution to the puzzle exists if you simply push the cork inside the bottle. Inside the bottle. Outside the box.

One of the great sports examples of thinking outside the box involves Red Auerbach and Larry Bird. By his junior year at Indiana State, Bird had a great reputation on the court. Auerbach and the Celtics, in a brilliant move, actually drafted Bird after his junior year, knowing full well that they would not have access to his talent for another twelve months. Only later would the genius of that "outside the box" move become apparent to most of the rest of us.

* * *

Try picking up the sports page from today's paper. If you hold the paper too close, just a couple of inches from your eyes, it doesn't work because the print is out of focus. Now try changing your perspective by moving the paper about twelve to fifteen inches away from your eyes. That simple change in perspective makes the message much clearer. With that in mind, never be afraid to view a challenge from a different perspective. Change the angle of your view, and your perspective, like a football scout who sits high up in the remote section of the stadium. Don't be afraid to think in ways that are contrary to the crowd, and stand apart from the majority view. Your investment decisions will have more clarity, and you may just enjoy the scenery.

Think for yourself, even if that means sometimes analyzing outside the box, and then make your move. Analysis time is like time in the huddle, and action time is the actual running of the play. Both are key to the success of the operation. Analysis without action is like a simulated video game, but action without analysis is like a blind pass into heavy traffic. Action is the great link between the "analysis" and the "outcome," so when you see a clear possibility, have the confidence and the drive to pursue it. Take the shot. Swing the bat. Throw the pass.

The fact is, many of the greatest teams and greatest coaches in history won no more than 60% to 70% of their contests over complete seasons. The 1961 Yankees won 67%, the 1975 Reds won 67%, and the 2002 Lakers won 71%. These teams were champions, and remain fan favorites, with players like Mickey Mantle, Johnny Bench, and Shaquille O'Neill. But in fact, they only won about two out of every three during what historians would call spectacular seasons. We place this emphasis on a 60% to 70% winning percentage for a couple of reasons. First, a similarity exists in the fact that over a very long period of market history, the U.S. stock market has gone up 71% of the time on an annual basis. The S&P 500 Index has actually increased fifty-five out of seventy-seven years (71% of the time) during the period 1926 through 2002. Secondly, we make this comparison because, when it comes to your investment plan, a winning percentage of 60% to 70% can lead to very positive net results. Let's look inside the numbers.

Consider a hypothetical series of ten investment trials that includes six wins (60%) and four losses (40%). Assume that the initial investment for each trial is a constant $10,000. Assume that four out of the ten trials result in a loss of 9% and the other six investment trials result in a gain of 22%. The 40% failure rate may concern you, but with the positive impact of the 60% success rate, how would you come out?

4 trials at -9% = -36%

6 trials at +22% = +132%

+96% divided by 10 trials = +9.6% average return per trial

The end result is that, even though your failure rate was 40%, you would finish these ten trials with a positive average return over each of the ten trials of 9.6%.

Outcomes like these prove that you do not have to be a genius when it comes to stock entry decisions. You do not need to bat anywhere in the neighborhood of a perfect one thousand in order to be successful. Like many of the great teams and coaches in sports history, you can be a successful, profitable investor with a win ratio of 60% to 70%, provided that you always show up, use rational position boundaries, and use defined exit strategies. You are a gamesman, so you know how the strategy works. You can give up your "pawns and rooks," as long as you protect your "bishops and queen." If you're humble enough to accept small manageable losses, you can last a long time and put a lot of points on the board by being a lot less than perfect.

In a football game, there are approximately 150 plays. Our studies show that the difference between winning and losing a particular game hinges, on average, on a minimum of two plays and a maximum of five; and of course, at any time, at any place on the field, it may hinge on one.

Vince Lombardi

Legendary Football Coach

Career achievement records are built one game at a time, and one decision at a time. Lombardi knew that the outcome of a game could be determined by two or three plays, or even worse, by only one significant play at exactly the wrong (or right) moment. His career record, like most of the great ones, was built as much by avoiding big losers as much as it was by creating big winners.

• • •

Since you're a sports fan, you know who they are, even if we don't mention most of them by name. They are the franchise owners in professional sports who wanted to win now. They wanted success "now," or at some present moment, even if it threatened the long-term success equation for their team. Owners with this mindset are into immediate gratification in a big way, and they sometimes curiously prefer to go all out for the Super Bowl "this" year, rather than set their franchises up to make the play-offs year after year after year.

The sad reality is that some investors have a similar mindset. On the golf course, or at some other social setting, they like to be able to talk about their last great kill (profit). They have little regard for the long-term foundation of their franchise. Like a big game hunter, they live for the thrill of the kill, and immediate gratification, and often end up suffering through extreme performance peaks and valleys. We all know of guys who took too much sector risk in technology and telecommunications companies in the late 1990s. By becoming extremely over-weighted in one or two sectors of the market, they behaved like the sports franchise owners who bet all the marbles on one or two franchise players, or one or two seasons. Sooner or later an overly concentrated strategy like that is bound to fail, and when it does they're left holding the bag.

For a minute, let's assume that you are a mega-millionaire, and you own an NFL franchise. Assume that you can see five years into the future. Would you rather, (a) make it to the Super Bowl this year, and then not even make the playoffs in each of the next four years; or (b) make the playoffs every year for the next five years, and by so doing, have a respectable chance of advancing deep into the playoffs every season, or of even winning it all?

I suppose it depends on your definition of success. Although it's a tough question in a pentium world like ours, a case can be made that the consistency of a team that makes the playoffs every year is the best choice. Consistent strength that leads to a high probability of making the playoffs every year is a great thing. Ask any coach who values his job.

If you make the playoffs every year, then you are among the best of the best. Your portfolio will score well when compared to your peers, and you will consistently set your team up for a run at the ultimate prize, and it isn't that what the game is all about, anyway?

Don't let short-term greed destroy your chances for long-term success. Push hard, then rest and repair, with a high regard for your long-term condition and the future success that it can bring to you. A strong understanding that superior performance "over time" is not the same thing as superior performance "all the time" will shelter you from a boom to bust experience in the markets.

In the end, what is the most important performance measurement, "relative performance" or "absolute performance?" Here's one way to attack the question. In the NHL, if the average number of goals scored per game last season was four, and your team only scored an average number of 2.5 per game, your team had a problem. On the other hand, if the average number of goals scored per game was one, and your team scored an average number of 2.5 per game, your team was "relatively" strong, and may have even had home ice advantage throughout the playoffs. A strong case can be made that performance comparisons should measure performance "relative" to some meaningful peer group.

If the market index went up 10% last year, and your portfolio went up only 4%, you had a problem. On a relative basis, you underperformed the market. On the other hand, if the market index went down 5%, and your portfolio went up only 4%, you look like a hero. Any absolute performance reading is only a number, and only half the story. The real deal is relative performance over time. Superior performance over time does not equal superior performance all the time. You do not have to win every weekend series in order to have a record of superior performance over time. Focus instead on fundamental strategies that give you opportunities to exhibit relative strength greater than your peers, and greater than the other teams in the league.

CHAPTER SEVENTEEN:

A DIFFERENT KIND OF E.S.P.

By being involved in the markets since John Madden was the head coach of the Raiders, and Joe Morgan was an all-star second baseman with the Reds, my experience has given me great confidence in an investment approach that is based upon a blend of three distinct academic subjects. In the following section, we take a look at the interaction of "economics, statistics, and psychology," in the search for stock market superiority. Call it "E.S.P." if you want to, as we explore the importance of some of the fundamental principles of economics, statistics, and psychology, and how they interact in the search for superior investment performance.

The intelligent always consider benefit and harm.

Sun-Tzu

Ancient Chinese Military Leader

The E in E.S.P.: Economics

Sun-Tzu would have been a great professor of many subjects, including the principles of economics. When you break things down, aren't most of life's tough decisions really about benefit versus harm, or risk versus reward, two of the most fundamental economic concepts. Econ is not a four-letter word, but rather, a study critical in the understanding of some of the most basic market success strategies.

Regardless of what you thought of your "Principles of Economics 101" professor in college, a solid understanding of basic economic principles such as risk versus reward, and supply versus demand, will always be valuable to you in the marketplace.

Remember, this writer is a guy who was a part of the slide-rule generation. The first Texas Instruments business calculator that I bought as a college student in the early 1970s cost more than $90. The tools for analysis change, but the basic economic principles remain the same.

Even though the fundamental relationships do not change, let's view and review some of the constant economic commandments from a new perspective. What if we were to view the ongoing battle between supply and demand for any stock (or any other real asset, for that matter) like the battle between two college football teams? Just as the stronger team takes control of the position on the field, the stronger economic force, either supply or demand, takes control of prices over short periods of time. Then, over the course of the game, the stronger force tends to dominate the action, which leads to more defined long-term price moves.

The year was . . .?

Lakers defeat Knicks for NBA title
FedEx is founded
The Godfather is Best Picture
A's win World Series over Reds
Cost of a first-class postage stamp is $.08
Dow Jones Industrial Average closes the year at 1,020

The year was . . . 1972.

If the buying demand for a sporting event increases because of some special circumstances (conference championship game) and the supply of tickets remains constant, then the price for tickets to that event should increase due to the primary principles of supply and demand. Supply remains relatively constant because of the limited seating in the stadium, but demand increases for the special event (a championship game), so prices increase. Recognizing the reasons for the increase can help determine the relative value of the deal for you. On the other hand, you may have at one time held extra tickets for some popular sporting event or concert. The minute the event started, the prevailing price probably dropped hard. The supply of tickets did not change, but the public demand for those tickets declined, so the going price for those tickets quickly moved in the same direction. At that point, supply won the battle over demand.

As mentioned in detail in the offensive strategy section, I prefer to call supply-demand analysis simply "demand analysis." In the football stadium, the supply of seats for any particular game remains relatively constant. The factor that changes most dramatically, based on surrounding sentiment and events, is demand for the seats. Similarly, even though mergers, acquisitions, and share buy-back programs take place, the supply of shares in the U.S. marketplace remains relatively steady over any given season. Demand is the more volatile variable, and is therefore a more important part of the current equation. If you get a handle on the impact of "demand" you will get a handle on the justification for market price increases and decreases.

Admittedly, as the factors that impact supply and demand increase in number, it gets tougher to pick up their signals. Go back to the college football game analogy. The action on any particular play is a sum of the collective action of all twenty-two players who are on the field for that play. Imagine that the current price of "North American Sporting Goods" stock is $50, and relate that to a current field position that places the ball exactly on the fifty-yard line. If a play takes place, and the forces of the offense and the defense (supply and demand) remain in balance, then the stock price will remain on the $50 line (50-yard line). When the equilibrium is eventually broken, the stronger force will take control of the direction and movement of the ball.

In this symbolic battle, the public address announcer, the cheerleaders, and the other noise factors in the stadium are of little significance. What really matters is the mental and physical prowess of the two teams (supply and demand) on the field for any specific play. Everything else in the stadium (marketplace) is practically insignificant when compared to the power of the supply team and the demand team.

On Wall Street, the constant battle between supply and demand is often described as the battle between the "bulls" and the "bears." The symbol of the bull, and terms like bullish, bullish sentiment, and bullish trends, are used to define periods of relatively strong demand and positive, advancing price trends. On the other hand, the symbol of the bear, as well as terms like bearish, bearish sentiment, and bearish trends, are used to define periods of relatively weak demand and negative, declining stock prices. A bearish period is one when supply of shares outstanding at current price levels seems to overpower demand, so prices trend lower in order to find some economic equilibrium point.

Even though you will never know all of the reasons why a specific stock is in a specific bullish or bearish trend, you can always use demand analysis to take a high-resolution picture of the economic forces that are affecting its current price. The process evolves like a journey down a previously undiscovered road. The road conditions five miles back or five miles ahead are of little significance to you. What matters is the current picture. The things that matter are the road signs you see right now that help define the conditions around you right now. You don't have to be an expert at forecasting the future, but you do need a clear focus when it comes to reading the road signs and other signals that are immediately in front of you. At any point along the way, the road signs of demand analysis will give you direction regarding current traveling conditions, and how to proceed in the most prudent manner. Obviously, a sign that reads "slow—curves ahead" has a different meaning from a sign that reads "speed limit 70 m.p.h." As you experience the journey known as stock market investing, the bullish and bearish signs that the market gives you will take on a clearer meaning. Just as the disciplined driver takes note of the various signs of the road, the disciplined investor takes note of all the supply and demand clues of the marketplace, and does so in a way that would make his Economics 101 professor proud.

The bottom line regarding economics in the marketplace goes something like this. Supply and demand forces create inefficiencies. This is a wonderful thing, because they create great opportunities for profit for the investor who can capitalize on these inefficiencies. The market is always right, because at any moment it represents the composite force of all supply and demand (selling and buying) for a specific asset. It is not always efficient, but it is always right. There is a difference. The market is neither good or bad, but the inefficiency displayed in a market price can be a huge advantage for the disciplined, focused, contrary investor.

* * *

The S in E.S.P.: Statistics

Life is pretty much a percentage business. It isn't making mistakes that is critical. It's correcting them and getting on with the principal task.

Donald Rumsfeld
U.S. Secretary of Defense

We would agree that statistics involves the study of numbers and data. If the money game is a numbers game, then a clear understanding of statistics can help bring more order to that game, so let's take a minute to recap some of the basics. After all, we are attempting to get a leg up on the competition by quantifying uncertainty, and that's where the study of statistics becomes beneficial.

We know that "probability" is the relative possibility that an event will occur. In sports, we often refer to probability as the odds, or the chances of a specific outcome.

In the study of statistics, the "mean" is the average value of a set number of observations. As examples, recall that the mean (average) number of plays in a NFL game is approximately 150, and the mean (average) annual return of the S&P 500 over the past eighty years is approximately 10.7%.

The "median," by comparison, is the midpoint of the data, which can be compared to the median in the center of an interstate highway. It often differs from the mean, as shown in the following example. Suppose a football team completes exactly ten passes in a particular game. Nine of these plays result in a gain of ten yards. The tenth pass ends exactly at the yard of scrimmage, so it nets zero yards. When analyzing the yardage gained on these ten completions, how would the mean and the median in this set of data compare with each other?

Nine completions, each for ten yards; one completion for zero yards; ten data points. The "mean" for this set of data equals nine yards, which is the average number of yards gained on each of the ten plays. The "median," on the other hand, which is the midpoint in the range of data points, equals five (the midpoint between ten yards and zero yards). In this example, most of us would agree that the mean is the more meaningful number. It represents a statistical average that most sports fans can identify with. The median, on the other hand, gives us a feel for how wide the range of data points is, but is sometimes skewed by data points far removed from the norm.

While stats can be a great tool, be aware that the blind use of statistics may not always be logical. As an example, let me first give you the answer to a specific question: "seventy degrees." Now consider the following input; you have one foot in a bucket of fifty degree water, and you have the other foot in a bucket of ninety degree water. What is the mean? What is the median? While the mean and the median are both seventy degrees, a nice average number, would you be comfortable with the situation? Absolutely not.

Life usually grants us statistical "independence," which means that the outcome of any specific event is not dependent on the one just before it, or just after it, or any other trial, for that matter. Each stands alone and is independent. If the stats show that Drew Bledsoe has a completion record of 60%, that is a valid statistic. However, just because his last six passes were complete, that fact does not lead to the conclusion that his next pass "must" be an incompletion. Since each event is independent of every other event, the probability of success on each pass remains 60%, and is free and independent of the ones that surround it.

The variance in a set of trials (data) is measured by a term known as the standard deviation. For many participants in the market, the main statistical fact to focus on is that the higher the standard deviation, the wider the variance in a specific set of data. A historically high standard deviation signals volatility rather than consistency in a set of data.

At this point, it is appropriate to dig into the real, yet subtle, differences between "variance of returns" and "risk of principal." Variance of returns is a fact of life in the capital markets. As shown below, it is common knowledge that stocks historically have a higher standard deviation (variance of returns) than either treasury bonds or treasury bills:

Period 1926-2001

Large company stocks	standard deviation 19.54	return 10.7%
Treasury bonds	standard deviation 6.81	return 5.3%
Treasury bills	standard deviation .90	return 3.8%

(source: Ibbotson and Associates)

Common thinking holds that risk is the possibility of a net loss of some personal asset, yet human nature often pushes us to take risk as a tradeoff in the pursuit of some positive outcome. In the capital markets, risk is often measured by using the statistical method known as standard deviation, which attempts to define a possible range of outcomes. These outcomes for the asset class known as common stocks include relatively larger possible increases and decreases in stock values, when compared with other classes of investment such as treasury bonds or treasury bills.

This is the point where the disciplined investor may avoid pain when compared to the passive investor who just puts his money away in an index fund. Just because the asset class has a wider variance in possible returns, the individual investor does not have to experience the ride created by that wider variance. The disciplined investor can use boundary limits and risk control techniques, like seatbelts and airbags, to insulate himself from some of the inherent variance in the asset class known as equities.

Variance in the periodic returns of any asset class does not necessarily equal risk of principal. If you keep that in mind, it will be easier for you to stay in the game. Virtually everything in the market and in life has some element of risk or sacrifice. If you stick with a game plan that allows you to generate returns in line with the market index, while at the same time incurring less variance than the market index, then you're getting somewhere. You're accomplishing your goals while experiencing more comfort and less volatility than the average, passive investor. The goal is genuine. Stay with it.

* * *

It's Not Personal. It's Probability.

Consider the following probability game. Assume you always start a card game with a total of five cards, three spades and two hearts. Assume that drawing one of the three spades is considered to be a "win," and drawing one of the two hearts is considered to be a "loss." The drawn card is returned to the hand of five after every trial, so a 40% failure rate (two hearts out of the five cards) is just a defined part of the game, as is a 60% success rate (three spades out of the five cards).

Now add real money. Assume you will win $10 every time you draw one of the spades, and you will lose $10 every time you draw a heart. What if you draw a heart the first time, add it back to the hand, shuffle the cards, and then draw a heart again on the second trial. You have just lost $20 in less than twenty seconds. Should you give up on the game at this point? No, because "probability theory" supports the fact that you will be successful over a larger number of trials. As stated earlier, the defined probability of success over a large number of trials in this game is 60%.

Probability theory dictates that you should win this card game in a session that included a large number of trials. In this five-card game, the previous draw means nothing, because every draw (trial) is independent of every other draw. Since each event is separate and distinct from those that precede it, as well as those that follow it, losing as many as six in a row does not change the defined 60% chance of winning the next (seventh) time.

Even the most rational players become anxious and frustrated when investment trials lead to failure several times in a row. When that happens to you (and it will happen to you), you may want to call a time out for a reality check. A real-world losing streak is generally not the time to push on like a sled dog. A more prudent course of action is to dial down a notch and mentally review exactly what is going on around you. Ask yourself some hard questions. Are you doing enough sound fundamental and technical homework? Are you sticking with quality, first-tier companies? Are you sticking with your predetermined position boundaries and entry levels? Are you sticking with your predetermined risk control techniques? In other words, are you sticking with the total game plan?

If there is a problem with the game plan, a mental timeout will help you identify it and take steps to correct it. There is nothing wrong with being less than fully invested while you rethink your approach. Take a little money off the table. Be like the coach who reviews films during the week in order to gain a clearer perspective regarding the strategy for next Sunday's game. Take a little time to recharge your thinking.

*   *   *

The P in E.S.P.: Psychology

> *All of our life is but a mass of small habits—practical, emotional, intellectual, and spiritual—that bear us irresistibly toward our destiny.*
>
> ***William James, M.D.***
> ***Father of Modern Psychology***

Before we go any further, let me say that we all should have studied harder in "Psych 101." I say this partly in jest, but the truth is that investor psychology may be the single most important variable that impacts stock prices in the free enterprise system known as the U.S. market. Let's take a look.

Many consider Phil Jackson to be the most successful coach in the history of the NBA, and his regular season winning percentage with the Lakers and the Bulls is around 74%. Every sports fan knows that he is one of the masters of the game, but did you know that Jackson received his B.A. degree from the University of North Dakota with a major in—you guessed it—psychology.

It is increasingly obvious that in both sports and investing, the psychology and mindset of the players are crucial to the formula for success. Early in your development as a serious investor it is critically important that you become aware of the market inside our head, which manifests itself as positive or negative mental energy toward any investment at any specific point in time.

In many ways the market is a psychological animal, so if we can remove ourselves from this animal just far enough to peacefully observe it, we can gain a better view. Accept the fact that the goal is to contain this animal, since you never will be able to totally control it. This animal is not good or evil, or right or wrong. It just is. Once you accept the market for the elusive, uncontrollable jungle animal that it is, you will become more grounded in the good news that the market cannot defeat you.

Granted, it's not easy to get inside the minds of other participants in the market, and you will never find psychological indicators discussed in a corporation's annual report. Nevertheless, you will be well served if you learn to recognize some of the indicators of mass psychology that undoubtedly impact the markets.

Emotions and Crowds

The observation has already been made that many individual investors are not rational, and since investor activity affects the market, it follows that the market is not rational. Even if you are a scientist or an engineer, you must simply accept the fact that there is no perfect equation or formula for success in the market. As much as we would like to compare the analytical power of the human brain to the personal computer, the breakdown in the comparison surfaces because human emotion interferes with logical response dynamics. Emotion will always remain an awesome, yet elusive force in the determination of investor decisions.

Emotionally, at any moment of our lives, we are either in a "down-trend," or we are in an "up-trend." Consider the following downward, defeatist spiral, since you may have been there yourself. Fear of making the wrong decision leads to poor judgment, which leads to unreasonable thinking, which leads to unreasonable decisions, which leads to more fear, and so on, and so on, and so on. How is a guy in this kind of predicament going to make any progress?

Now consider my own personal example of an upward spiral. In early 2001, a time when the U.S markets were really starting to struggle, I developed the idea for this book. As I recorded some ideas on paper, and further defined the details of the discipline that I use in my work, my confidence in the value that this work could provide to others increased. Even as some members of the financial community were spiraling down, my confidence led to more ideas, which led to more defined writing, which led to more confidence, which led to more ideas, which increased the upward spiral. I was living out the quote, "a professional writer is an amateur who did not quit."

Emotion regarding money issues is a lot like fire. The energy and power it generates can be extremely helpful, or it can lead to damage and destruction. It all depends on how it is controlled. In the end, your success will be directly related to your reading of mass emotions and mass psychology, and how you allow your personal mindset to battle against it. While you will never be able to control the markets, you can control your take on them in order to stay grounded emotionally. Work on blocking and tackling, and the basics of how emotions drive the other members of the crowd. At the same time work on neutralizing the flames of your own emotional fire with positive, productive activities that have nothing to do with business.

Although it is one of life's great emotions, "love" is a lousy emotion when it comes to your investment portfolio. Never fall in love with a stock, and never let an investment become a member of the family. A stock is an inanimate, intangible asset, period. There's an old saying in Texas that "everything I have, except my wife and children, is for sale (for the right price.)" Just because you love a company's product, or its reputation, don't be seduced into loving the stock. Emotional ties like that can cloud your good judgment, and limit it when you may need it the most.

> *When dealing with people, remember that you are not dealing with creatures of logic, but with creatures of emotion.*
>
> ***Dale Carnegie***
> ***Author, Motivator***

We are blessed to live in the comfort of the twenty-first century. The path of least resistance often attracts us to stylish cars and stylish gadgets, and the favored sports team rather of the underdog. If we follow the crowd, and follow the herd, life seems to be easier because we don't have to analyze and agonize over contrary decisions.

No one is thinking if everyone is thinking alike.

Gen. George S. Patton Jr.
World War II General

You will never have any control over the psychology of the other participants in the market. Sure, you might tell a few friends about a specific stock. Someday you might even write an investing newsletter, or host an investing radio show, but even then you will never exert much control over crowd psychology and the opinions of the masses. The ocean of information and opinions regarding the market is just too vast.

Crowd psychology often shows up in our support for the hot sports teams. Nationwide, two of the most popular sports teams in recent years have been the Lakers and the Yankees. They win, so fair weather fans support them, so they become more popular, so more fans support them, and so on. At the same time, the crowd favors the hot movie, or the hot rock band, since the average person feels most comfortable in a crowd, even if the crowd is wrong.

Now let's consider the story from another angle. The truth is, we should be ever grateful for crowd influence and crowd psychology, because it is extreme crowd psychology that leads to inefficiencies in the marketplace. If the stock superstore was a perfectly efficient place, every player would make the same amount of money. We all know this is not the case, which is a great realization for the reasonable investor who has the strength to keep his own emotions in check, and avoid being influenced by the crowd. Profits can come to those who recognize that inefficiencies are always going to exist in a free and open marketplace.

If the majority of stock investors were always right, the majority of stock investors would be rich. Since money moves with emotions, it is actually very wise to remove yourself from the crowd at extreme levels of optimism or pessimism. Assuming that investors put their money where their mouth (heart) is, if the majority of the crowd is bullish on a stock, then it follows that they have already made a bullish commitment to that stock. That said, what is left to spark the additional intense buying demand necessary to spike the stock to even higher levels? That's the problem, because in the real world strong buying demand may no longer exist. Like a wave that can only push so far before it relaxes and ebbs backwards, an intense stock move based upon extreme crowd psychology must sooner or later relax, and even retreat. For that reason, it is wise to avoid siding with the crowd if there is extreme emotion in the marketplace. If the big money controlled by the crowd has already moved into a position or out of a position, then while aligning with the crowd may feel good, it may be the wrong thing to do. It may be better to be a little contrary, go it alone, and pack your own parachute.

> *Pack your own parachute*
>
> **Anonymous**

Be forewarned that this will not be easy, because at times of extreme market emotion, the media is often cheering for the wrong side of the market. Near the end of bear markets, popular news magazines have been known to print a picture of a bear on the cover, or to exhibit headlines relating to the end of equities. These extreme clues may actually signal that the most extreme selling pressure is already on the table, and reflected in the current price levels. Assuming that you have built up cash buying power because of your take on previous market signals, it may be time to become more proactive and positive because of the fear and hesitancy of others.

To view the other side of the story, near the end of the great bull market of the late 1990s, most of the thinking of the popular crowd was still very positive. Even though comparative valuations were off the charts, many publications boasted of the "new paradigm," and the fact that "this time it is different." History shows that the contrary investor, who became cautious and took defensive actions as the market started to roll over in the spring and summer of 2000, was doing the right thing. At the time though, that was about 180 degrees removed from what the crowd was reading in the popular press.

If you can keep your head when all about you are losing theirs, yours is the earth and everything that's in it.

Rudyard Kipling
Author, Poet

There you have it. Crowds sometimes go mad in masses. As a prudent investor, be ever thankful for the force we know as crowd psychology, because it provides the fuel that fires inefficient moves in market prices. This phenomenon can create great opportunities for those who remove themselves from the fire, and take actions slightly removed from the crowd. Don't get me wrong. In many ways the force of crowd psychology is a wonderful thing, because of the inefficiencies and the opportunities that it creates. Recognize it and respect it, just don't get caught up in it.

CHAPTER EIGHTEEN:

WAS IT SPORTS OR SPORTS PSYCHOLOGY?

UCLA. Notre Dame. Ohio State. These great universities all have sports psychologists on staff in their athletic departments. Many PGA tour golfers now work regularly with psychological consultants. Over the past ten years, baseball stars like Mark McGwire and John Smoltz made public their work with sports psychologists, and the positive results that came from it.

The American Psychological Association Division 47 defines "sports psychology" as "the scientific study of the factors associated with participation and performance in sport, exercise, and other types of physical activity."

Physical factors have always been a given, but the mental factors have become increasingly important to the modern athlete. In fact, if we were to poll contemporary Olympic athletes regarding the keys to success, it would not be surprising to find that mental factors now weigh in more heavily than physical factors.

Modern sports psychologists realize that talent and physical training can only take an athlete so far. At some point, a trained mind becomes an asset that can enhance performance, assist in overcoming the pressures of competition, and take the athlete to the next level. Thus, a discipline has evolved over the last generation that focuses on factors such as the mindset and the mental attitude of the athlete. The focus of modern sports psychology has grown from infancy to maturity, and now includes specific subsets such as concentration strategies, relaxation techniques, and positive imagery exercises.

It is agreed that sports psychology is the study of factors that enhance performance, so in its simplest form, it is the psychology of performance. With that foundation, it follows that the psychology of investment performance, or "investment psychology," may involve many of the same human elements.

Now we're getting someplace. A case can be made that sports psychology and investment psychology are as related as Ken Griffey and Junior. Since investor psychology is the study of how psychology influences investor choices, it ultimately affects investor performance. Since investor performance is important to all of us, the study can help us recognize biases and blind spots, and get us closer to our "A" game as career investors.

> *Nothing can stop the man with the right mental attitude from achieving his goal; nothing on earth can help the man with the wrong mental attitude.*
>
> ***Thomas Jefferson***
> ***Third U.S. President***

The secret to your success in the market will never be found in the market, but rather in you, and in your mental makeup, and in your mental approach to the market. Since we all agree that athletes who make it to the NBA or the NFL have superior talent, the difference between the very good and the great is that intangible we call mental toughness. In their minds, the best of the best are so tough they think they have won the game before it even starts.

When you study the action between the white lines, the one who excels is often the one who trains a little differently when it comes to the mental side of the game. Think about the gold medal Olympic athlete. Great athletes often train in some almost quirky way that is mentally and physically just a little bit removed from the crowd They have a special spark in their eyes, and they continually stretch toward not one set of goals, but redefined and reworked goals. As a result, the zone they are searching for is more of a "stretch zone" than a "comfort zone."

The year was . . .?

Terry Bradshaw was #1 pick in NFL draft

Orioles defeat Reds in the World Series

Monday Night Football debuts

Patton wins Academy Award for Best Picture

Construction of the World Trade Center is begun

Dow Jones Industrial Average closes year at . . . 839

The year was . . . 1970.

As you prepare psychologically for the investing experience, your training may in some ways compare to the preparation of the serious martial arts competitor, where focus and discipline before the competition keep the competitor in a grounded mental state during the heat of the competition. When you follow the same path as an investor, your actions will be more reasoned and predictable, with higher lows and lower highs. Your mind doesn't have to be "in flow," but if you can get to that point, that's all the better. The mental training you rehearse before the turmoil of a specific market moment will make your thinking clearer when the whistle blows.

A master is the one who stays on the mat five minutes longer every day than everyone else.

Martial Arts Saying

A few years ago a casual wear clothing company promoted the slogan, "no fear." What a simply great mantra for today's serious investor. You see, the human mind has only a limited capacity for processing information. If you are preoccupied with fear and worry, you have less capacity available to help you perform effectively in the other areas of your life. Fear of failure can definitely keep you out of the game.

The "hard drive" known as your mind only has so much processing space. If too much of it is taken up with fear of future outcomes, then that limits your ability to think and learn and rationally process other decisions. Why not keep your mental hard drive free from clutter. Adversity is a part of every game of our lives, but have "no fear." At the very least, have less fear, and concentrate on what you can control.

The reality is that markets feel great at the top and lousy at the bottom. Trust me, I've been there. That fact will no longer be a major problem for you, because now you know that the market is not about feeling good or bad, anyway.

It's totally normal for RSIs (rookie stock investors) to experience a mental honeymoon period when making new stock investments. On opening day every team is in first place, right? Everything is good on opening day, so the rookie makes "buy" decisions based on hope, greed, and the fact that people he knows probably own the same investment. He's still comfortable in the crowd, and he hasn't experienced the gut-wrenching regret of either a big loss, or a big gain that turned into no gain.

After major market up-trends, those who missed the boat and didn't participate often follow the crowd because they are worried about missing further gains. At the height of a speculative bubble, sometimes they even buy for no reason other than "everybody else is buying." Positive money flows go into the mutual funds with the best track records, because they are usually the ones receiving the most positive ink in the financial press.

After the bubble has burst, RSIs tend to make delayed sell decisions (or what may be called "sell indecisions," the lack of sell decisions) based on fear and hate. Their stocks have started to roll over, the financial press has turned more negative, and it is no longer as much fun to discuss stock market war stories. Sometimes the market moves as fast as a Texas tornado, and sometimes it acts more like a slow drought that chokes off profits day by day. Either way, the mental pressure on rookies often becomes so severe that they throw in the towel by selling near the bottom. Tired of the ridicule and remorse that they associate with stock ownership, they sometimes abandon the cause and never come back.

Both sports and stocks are unpredictable, but your mindset never has to be. Since the market has no regard for you, the last thing you need to do is let it manipulate you by making you volatile and unpredictable. Adapt, decide, act, and then move on with confidence in your decisions. When it comes to your decision-making, it's okay to be red or green, but don't be gray. Decision is meaningless without action. Some of the best decisions you make will be made away from the noise, like those of a coach made in the quiet of the film room.

In the end, it's not the "action" of the market, it's your "reaction" to the market, and how you respond to what is served up to you. Control what you can, and direct all your analytical energy towards the prudent actions that you decide to take, knowing that your emotional stability is vastly more important than your level of raw intelligence. Keep your ego in check, knowing that the positives that result from your decisions are not the result of brilliance, but of discipline, quiet confidence, focus, and flexibility.

Checklist: The Special Teams

1. Do everything you can to neutralize your emotions regarding your investments. Seek higher emotional lows and lower emotional highs.
2. Your "reaction" to the market is much more important than the action of the market.
3. Suppress your ego. A big ego is of little value to the successful investor.
4. Your portfolio is not one big emergency. Avoid streaming quotes and streaming financial news.
5. The best umpires see it, call it, and move on. The best investors

do the same thing.

6. Define a time and a place to think away from the noise. Think slowly, act quickly.
7. Pack your own parachute.
8. Superior performance over time does not mean the same thing as superior performance all the time. Make decisions based upon a desire to achieve superior relative performance over time.
9. In the end, the "Economics" of supply and demand drive the markets.
10. A sound understanding of "Statistics," and probability theory, will benefit you.
11. "Psychology," in the form of investor sentiment, plays a key role in the ultimate supply and demand economics of the marketplace.
12. The success formula always includes failures.

* * *

At the major league level, fielding errors are a statistic that is recorded not only in the daily box scores, but also as a part of the permanent career history of every player. In the NFL, player mistakes on key plays are captured on film to be reviewed by coaches and critics time and time again—replay after replay.

Thank goodness for the fact that, in the games of money and markets, errors are private, and are not recorded in the financial box scores. Yet errors, missed assignments, and losses are a part of the experience, even for the great ones.

The years teach much which the days never know.

Ralph Waldo Emerson
Author

It's all right. You can live with that. Why? Because you're working on improving on the traits held by great athletes and great coaches. You're a work in progress. You're working on developing the discipline of a guy like Larry Bird, and the confidence of a guy named Joe Montana. You're working on developing the focus of a guy named Ted Williams, and the flexibility of a guy like Joe Gibbs.

You're working on an offense that you might call "West Coast," or "singles and doubles." It's one that a guy like Tony Gwynn (93% singles and doubles man) would be proud of.

You're working on a defense that Vince Lombardi would approve of, knowing that you don't need a lot of rules, you just need to keep the ones that you make.

You're working on the extras, the E.S.P. of investing, that a guy named Phil Jackson would be proud of. You know that success in the stock market has to do with more than finance textbooks and present value calculators. You know that it has to do with mental drive, mental sweat, and command over a controlled system of investing in an uncontrollable market.

* * *

Red Auerbach (Boston Celtics) coached teams that won nine NBA titles, yet he had a career regular season winning percentage of only 65%. Twenty years. Highs, lows, victories, defeats, failures, successes.

Scotty Bowman (Canadiens, Penguins, Sabres, Blues, Red Wings) coached NHL teams that won nine Stanley Cups, but he finished his career with a regular season winning percentage of only 65%. Thirty years. Highs, lows, victories, defeats, failures, successes.

Don Shula (Miami Dolphins, Baltimore Colts) coached teams that won two Super Bowls, yet over his entire career his teams won only 68% of their regular season games. Thirty-three years. Highs, lows, victories, defeats, failures, successes.

What a consistent statistic. What sports fan wouldn't jump at the chance to have dinner with any or all of these guys? Even though they are among the most respected coaches of all time, Auerbach, and

Bowman, and Shula all tasted defeat more than 30% of the time. Maybe that stat, more than any other, truly defines them as champions.

Errors, missed assignments, defeats—the only guarantee is that you will experience them in the stock market. The mistakes, like practice shots, are just a part of the process. Probability theory, and the long-term upward bias of the U.S. stock market, will remain tremendous allies for you if you remain disciplined, confident, focused, and flexible. The games you lose along the way will only get you closer to the victories. Like those guys named Auerbach, and Bowman, and Shula, you can lose a few along the way, and still become a true champion in every sense of the word.

"The years teach much which the days never know," according to Emerson. It now seems clear that:

The sporting experience is a series of mostly meaningless failures, interrupted by highly meaningful successes.

The investing experience is a series of mostly meaningless failures, interrupted by highly meaningful successes.

Wait a minute—isn't that the experience we call life? Maybe it really is the same game after all.

Index

Aaron, Hank, 36
Absolute Performance, 188
Active Management, 91
Air Travel, 63-64, 172
Ali, Muhammad, 63, 80
American Depository Receipts, 107-108
American Funds, 101
Anchoring, 159
Antelope, 90
Aristotle, 10, 163
AT&T, 80, 82
Attack Mode, 126, 129
Auerbach, Red, 211-212

Balance Mode, 127,129
Balance, 97
Baseball, 13-14, 21-22
Batting Average, 13-14, 21
Bear Market, 146
Berra, Yogi, 121
Bird, Larry, 8
Bloodlines, 151-152
Bonds, (Investment) 148-149
Bonds, Barry 148-149
Boundary Limits, 166
Boundary System, 133-134
Bowman, Scottie, 211-212
Bradshaw, Terry, 171
Brain, 34, 35
Brodeur, Martin, 66-67
Bull Market, 146
Buy and Hold, 42-43

Carnegie, Andrew, 100
Carnegie, Dale, 200
Cash, 149-150
Champagne, 164
Checklist, Defense, 91
Checklist, Offense, 165-166
Checklist, Special Teams, 209-210
Churchill, Winston, 28, 52, 75, 171
Cincinnati Reds, 185
Cisco Systems 43, 153
Coaches 7,11 134
Coco Cola, 109
Confidence, 19-21
Control Mode, 128-129
Control, 31, 174
Course Management, 75
Covey, Stephen, 32
Cowher, Bill, 51
Cromwell, Oliver, 163
Crowd Psychology, 201-203
Cut Losses, 51-52, 73

Debartolo Corp., 96
Decisions, 175
Defense, 91, 84
Defensive Coaches, 50-51
Defensive Driving, 49-50
Defined Exit Strategy, 51-52
Demand Analysis, 192-192
Denver Broncos, 37, 77
Disconnect, 80
Diversification, 97-102
Diversify, 165
Donahue, Terry, 96
Dow Jones Industrial Average, 147
Down-A-Lot Stock, 78-91
Dual Analysis, 165, 116-117, 119

Economic Sectors, 98-100
Economics, 189-192, 210, 121
Ego, 20, 209
Elevator Offense, 135-137, 139

Elevator System, 12-13, 165
Emerson, Ralph Waldo, 210
Emotions and Crowds, 199-200
Emotions, 209
Errors, 63, 171, 212
Events, 147
Events, Historic, 42

Failure, 22
Fear, 35, 165
Fidelity Magellan Fund, 101
Fifty Day Moving Average, 129-131
First Loss, 76
Flexibility, 37
Franchise Player, 156
Free Enterprise System, 35
Fundamental Analysis, 111-115

Game Plan, 65
Game, Investing, 45, 212
Game, Sporting, 45, 212
Garciaparra, Nomar, 8
General Manager, 96-97, 102
Gibbs, Joe, 38-39
Global 120 (G-120), 107-109, 115-116,
Goalies, 66-67
Golf, 75
Graphs, 119-121
Green Bay Packers, 9
Green Light, 126, 129
Gwynn, Tony, 15-16

Handicap, 40-41
Harvest Rules, 140-142
Harvest System, 165
Hockey, 66-67
Holy Grail, 111
Home Run, 68
Hope, 69, 82
How To Make Money In Stocks, 58
Hull, Brett, 18
IBM, 81

Investing Experience, 45, 212
Investor Types, 22-23

Jackson, Reggie, 5
James, William, M.D., 198
Jefferson, Thomas, 206
Jeter, Derek, 114
Johnson & Johnson, 114
Johnson, Jimmy, 18
Johnson, Spencer, M.D., 40
Journey, 34

Kill Your Losers, 54, 91
Kipling, Rudyard, 203
K-Mart, 152
Koufax, Sandy, 37-38
Kryzewski, Mike, 37

Landry, Tom, 50-51
Large Cap 100 (LC-100), 103-107
Larsen, Don, 143
Lennon, John, 181
Limit Order, 160
Livermore, Jesse, 54, 125, 159
Lombardi, Vince, 5, 9, 10, 186
Long Shots, 154
Los Angeles Lakers, 185

Madden, John, 183
Major League Baseball, 21
  Association, 121
Mantle, Mickey, 19
Marino, Dan, 5
Market Operating System (MOS), 65-
  66, 68, 91
Market Order, 160
Marshall, General George, 74
Martial Arts, 207
Mathematicans, 30
Matrix, Price to 200 Day Moving
  Average, 129
Mays, Willie, 79-80
Mean, 193, 194
Median, 194
Memory, 183
Mental Capacity, 34-35
Military Strategy, 82
Modern Portfolio Theory, 97-98
Money Market Funds, 149-150
Montana, Joe, 31-32
MOS (Market Operating System), 65-
  66, 68, 91
Moving Averages, 123-125

Napoleon, 27
NBA, 21
Negative Compounding, 85-87
New York Mets, 80
New York Yankees, 185
NFL, 31, 23
NHL, 66-67
No Fear, 207-208
No Man's Land, 153-154

Officials, 182-183
One-Decision Stocks, 82-91
O'Neill, William, 58
Operating Systems, 65-66
Outside The Box, 184
Over Diversification, 100-101

Pain, 56
Palmeiro, Raphael, 157
Parachute, 202
Pareto Principle, 140
Paterno, Joe, 19
Patton, General George, 18, 55, 201
Perfection, 62, 74, 91, 141-142
Performance (Stock) 41, 145
Piazza, Mike, 17
Play Book (Investing), 13
Player Selection, 96-97
Playing Field, 125-129
Poker, 30, 61-62
Porsche, 52
Powell, Colin, 34
Probability, 196-197
Procter & Gamble, 82
Pro. Tech. Analysis Assn., 121
Profits And Losses, 54
Psychology, 198-199, 210

Quality, 151-152
Quotes, Business leaders, 169-170

Reality TV, 31, 89-90
Red Light, 128
Regret, 31, 33, 164-165
Relative Performance, 188
Rice, Jerry, 11-12
Risk Management, 73
Risk Of Principal, 195
Risk, Measured, 44
Road Signs, 192-193
Roosevelt, Theodore, 70, 165
RSI (Rookie Stock Investor), 22-23, 33, 70, 152, 208
"Rule Of 72", 85
Ruth, Babe, 79-80
Ryan, Nolan, 5, 72
Rypien, Mark, 39

S & P 500 Index, 103-104, 143
Sailing, 44-45
San Francisco 49'ers, 95-96
Schultz, George, 90
Screening Techniques, 96
Sectors, Economic, 98-100
Self-Control, 71-72
Sell Discipline, 54-55
Sell-Stop Order, 56-59, 91
Shaw, Alan, 77-78
Shula, Don, 211-212
Signal, 166
Socrates, 95
Spielberg, Stephen, 182
Sporting Experience, 45, 212
Sports Psychology, 205-206
Stacking Formations, 130-131
Standard & Poor's Equity Index, 103-104, 143
Standard & Poor's Stock Reports, 112
Standard Deviation, 195
Statistical Independence, 194-195
Statistics, 193-195
Stengel, Casey, 83, 173
Stock Market Performance, 181-182
Stock Market University, 55
Stock Performance, 41, 145
Stock Quotes, 179-180
Stock Search, 115-116, 132
Stocks, 41
Stress, 176-177
Sun Tzu, 14, 39, 44, 189
Superior Performance, 188,210
Supply And Demand, 119, 190-191
Survivor, 89-90
Sweet Spot, 111

Systems, Investing, 19

Target Corp., 152-153
Technical Analysis, 111-112, 119-122
Theissman, Joe, 39
Thermostat, 24
Thoreau, Henry David, 17
Top-Down approach, 113
Trials, 21-22, 185-186
Trend Analysis, 121, 124
Tug-of-War, 76

U.S. Stock Market, 83
Umpires, 182, 209

Value Line Investment Survey, 112, 116
Variance Of Returns, 195-196
VSI (Veteran Stock Investor), 22-23, 29, 32, 34-35, 39, 44, 161

Walsh, Bill, 41
Wal-Mart, 82
Warner, Kurt, 135-136
Weapon (Investment), 71
Websites, Stock Screening, 115
Websites, Technical, 129-130
Who Moved My Cheese, 40
Williams, Doug, 39
Williams, Ted, 27-28
Winners And Losers, 53-54, 91
Wooden, John, 5, 29
Woods, Tiger, 7

Yellow Light, 127

Afterword

I am always interested in hearing from sports fans, coaches, and athletes who would like to share their perspective on sports and investing. If you would like more detail on the strategies described in this book, please contact me at ....

website:

www.itsallthesamegame.com

e-mail address:

NRTEXAS@COMCAST.NET

mail:

5700 Tennyson Parkway #650
Plano, TX 75024